⟩⟩⟩⟩⟩⟩ Cinema One

23 Theories of Film

Theories of Film

Andrew Tudor

The Viking Press
New York

The Cinema One series is published by
The Viking Press, Inc., in association with
Sight and Sound and the Education
Department of the British Film Institute.

Published in 1974 in a hardbound and paperbound
edition by
The Viking Press, Inc.,
625 Madison Avenue, New York, N.Y. 10022

SBN 670–69811–3 (hardbound)
SBN 670–01965–8 (paperbound)

Library of Congress catalog card number: 73–8380

Printed and bound in Great Britain

Contents

Cover: *A Fistful of Dynamite* (Sergio Leone)

Hitchcock: *Vertigo* and *Frenzy* (top); Hawks: *Bringing Up Baby*

1: Introduction

Recent years have seen a developing interest in serious study of the cinema. The range and number of close analyses of the work of particular directors and studies of special aspects of film has increased, it sometimes seemed, day by day. In the face of this burgeoning obsession it is thus a little odd that film theory, classically defined by Eisenstein, has remained much as it was: a little practised and barely reputable pursuit. Though we may now take seriously a Howard Hawks or an Alfred Hitchcock,[1] to 'theorize' about film still smacks of over-intellectualism. It is one thing to recognize the need to reflect self-consciously on the critic's 'tools of the trade'; it is another to indulge. In some part this is a consequence of the traditional Anglo-Saxon mistrust of such a suspiciously European pursuit. English thinking, and not only on film, has seemingly always preferred to keep its feet firmly planted on the ground, a policy which has not been without its rewards. But on the debit side it has also led to a situation wherein the larger intellectual environment has barely felt the need to address itself to the cinema. Even now our orthodox academic institutions lack a context in which to study the major new art of the twentieth century

1. See, for example, Robin Wood, *Hitchcock's Films*, A. Zwemmer Ltd., London, 1965, and *Howard Hawks*, Secker and Warburg/B.F.I., London, 1968.

as anything more than some sort of sociological curiosity. Academic aesthetics has concerned itself with more 'profound' and 'genuine' arts.

This belief that film aesthetics is not quite respectable has had various consequences. As I shall go on to amplify, such antagonism pressured attention away from Eisenstein's 'scientific' and general interest in a theory of film and toward a *defensive* need to justify the new 'art'. Much of the effort which might have gone toward extending our understanding of the new medium has instead been poured into the bottomless pit of aesthetic respectability. The proposition that Film was indeed Art haunted a whole generation of critics and was to set a limit on their ambitions and on their contribution. Because of such outside social and intellectual pressures – the intellectual antagonism was socially supported – we have inherited a culture of film with a vacuum at the centre. Seventy-five years of history have left us with no unified body of knowledge on which to draw; no consistent set of terms to employ. Other than in the precariously surviving specialist journals film criticism remains even now a fundamentally dilettantish pursuit. The critic of one English Sunday paper recently implied that Hitchcock had only been in the business some eighteen years in which time he had made less than a dozen films. The film under review had already received publicity as his fiftieth feature! In magnitude this is atypical; in trend it is all too common.

It can hardly be the intention of this book to fill such a 'gap', even in its theoretical aspect. Optimistically assuming that such changes do come about, they will be many years in the making. But this book *does* ask that we give some portion of our expanding energies to the particular area of development very broadly defined as 'theory' of film. That we not only take films seriously; we look likewise to the history of critical writings. Elia Kazan, in a bitter moment, accused film critics of being eunuchs; of writing about what they were unable to do. To press the analogy further is to recollect that the eunuchs frequently played a crucial role in their world and, while I would not wish to defend all against Kazan's charge, I would surely wish to defend some. Perhaps this survey of some of the chief eunuchs will demonstrate quite why. At least it might help in the task of definition; in understanding where we are, how we got there, and what we might need to get any further. It is to this preliminary aim of clarification that I direct the exegesis and criticism which follow. To build on such a basis is the task of another day.

Theories of Theories

Most obviously we have to begin by asking what constitutes a theory of film. In a sense this whole book offers an answer. But in a more limited way there is some use in putting the question specifically. In particular, what has traditionally been meant by the phrase 'theory of film'? Now there are two well-known books of precisely this title, but neither of them is clear as to the 'theory' in question. The one, by Bela Balazs, is a collection of general and often rather dated fragments only tenuously interlinked. The other, by Siegfried Kracauer, is a massively desperate attempt to justify realist cinema as aesthetic perfection. The one thing they do have in common – in retrospect the lowest common denominator of their 'theories' – is a desire to make *general* statements about the cinema. To advance propositions which transcend particular films and thence apply to film in general. Like Eisenstein, Balazs expresses it at its strongest in his avowed interest in the 'intrinsic laws of development' of the art, though in practice, also like Eisenstein, he leaves such laws unspecified.

Minimally, then, the expression 'theory of film' has been applied to any attempt to make general assertions about the medium. Much everyday usage corresponds to this meaning. Any critic concerned to talk about characteristics of the medium as well as about particular movies has been labelled, for good or ill, a theorist, a terminology which is clearly far too vague. While generalization is undoubtedly a necessary component of 'theory', all generalizations do not therefore constitute theories. A theory is not simply the sum total of our general knowledge of a subject; its functions are not exhausted in the presentation of *ad hoc* sets of assertions linked only in that they all apply to film. It has, in its way, a creative character of its own. By explicitly linking together its various components we are made aware of relationships and regularities which would not otherwise be apparent. We are able to clarify, for example, the links between conceptions of film editing and of film acting, and their joint consequences for the process of film communication. The classic Russian arguments about *typage* and *montage* involve just such links.

This enables us to further pin down the notion of film theory. It is not simply a question of the generality of our statements, of their status as presumptive 'laws' which always hold true. There is also an issue of method involving the *systematization* of our thought. The film theorist is distinguished from the film essayist (who might also make general statements) by his stress on the systematic. To theorize is, of necessity, to invoke the criterion of logical consistency, and so logically to interrelate various diverse elements into theories. As a body of such theory is formed, each stage in its development gives us a new vantage point on our subject. It provides a different pair of spectacles, a different 'theoretical framework', much as, for example, the collective propositions of Newtonian mechanics historically offered a new perspective on the dynamics of moving bodies. At root, our every act of observation invokes some implicit framework; to theorize is to make such a framework explicit so that it might be explored for cracks. Given all this there is still obviously a range of meanings of 'theory'. At one end there is the minimal demand that writers on film render explicit their assumptions. At the other extreme a maximal demand that we must work toward formulating a general and systematic body of empirically tested knowledge about film; in effect, a science of film. Recent years have seen a fairly widespread critical demand for 'minimal' theory: the breakdown in communication between different 'schools' has made such a need evident to a wide range of interested parties. This has inevitably led to a more philosophically developed discussion of cinema. On the other hand, 'maximal' theory has become increasingly hived off into outside specializations. From the era of Eisenstein, whose intention it was to create a mighty, overarching, scientific theory of film, we have come to the age of the specialist. Eisenstein attempted to invoke his own psychology, sociology, and film 'linguistics'. For him the impetus came from a central concern with film. Now the psychologists, sociologists, and linguists fragment the subject into its disciplinary variants. For them the impetus is extra-cinematic. At its most general, one task of 'maximal' theory could be to reunite these elements.

It should be clear that I am using 'theory' in a fairly general way. It would obviously be possible to limit the term quite drastically; in some circumstances it might even be essential. Thus, 'theory' could be conceived as part of a process of hypothesis formulation, testing, and, if necessary, reformulation on the basis of empirical materials. In short, the application of 'scientific method' to the task of expanding our knowledge of film. But most people do not limit 'theories of film' in this way, and this book is primarily concerned with what *is* and only partially with what *ought* to be. Much of what has passed as theory of film has really been an attempt to lay bare the assumptions and arguments which have underlain certain critical practices. Bazin, Kracauer, the 'auteur theory', are cases in point. They are elaborations of particular critical 'world-views', special frameworks for the analysis of films. They can hardly be by-passed as not constituting theory proper, for we have much to learn from them.

This enlarged area of interest brings with it its own

11

particular problems. We are to be concerned with theoretical frameworks employed for a range of purposes and deriving from a number of disciplinary viewpoints. One difference, in particular, needs attention. It is possible to study film in order, *primarily*, to understand the empirical operation of the medium, or, *primarily*, as a basis for making judgements of quality. Evidently, the clearer our understanding the better the factual basis on which our judgements are founded; equally (believers in the myth of 'objective criticism' apart) our 'scientific' study could not be conducted in an evaluative vacuum. But there is a definite distinction of aim between the two, and their confusion can be, at the very least, misleading. Eisenstein, as I shall discuss, is sometimes dismissed as guilty of aesthetic monomania: of offering *montage* as the ultimate aesthetic arbiter of taste. In fact, he was much more concerned with *montage* as part of a theory of *how film in fact affected people*, than with making all-pervasive judgements of value. For the want of terms I shall refer to the former interest as developing a *model* of film, to the latter as developing an *aesthetic* of film. The intertwining of such interests has elsewhere caused the exact status of propositions to become confused. Bazin, for example, argued that *Citizen Kane* was a film of high quality in that it was a film of realism. Realism was an axiom of his *aesthetic* position. But the statement which links this axiom with the specific aesthetic judgement of *Citizen Kane* raises problems. The realism of the film, Bazin argues, derives from its use of deep-focus photography and minimal cutting. Such techniques minimize fragmentation of the real world. The trouble is that this could be a *definition* of realism as non-fragmentation, or an assertion that films employing such techniques are *perceived* as more real. The latter, unlike the former, is open to empirical test, although Bazin uses it as a self-evident aesthetic judgement. Thus, although there is nothing inherently wrong with the argument, it does involve different sorts of statements with consequent different criteria of adequacy. Such shifts should be made clear, though they seldom are.

This leads to a working distinction between theories which are aimed principally at scientific comprehension of film – what I have referred to as *models* of film – and theories aimed at principally making evaluative judgements – what I have termed *aesthetics* of film. Historically the emphasis in film writings has been in the *aesthetic* direction, in effect, with the provision of a rationale for statements of the form 'I like this' or 'film should be like that'. Clearly some body of aesthetic argument of an abstract theoretical nature could be inferred from the work of any critic, whether or not the resulting case was consistent or even plausible. For example, Robin Wood's critical studies can be shown to derive from the kind of moral arguments advanced by the Leavisite school of literary criticism. To argue this is not, as Alan Lovell has demonstrated, simply scholastic; it enables us to better understand the basis on which the critic's practice rests.[2] Without at least mutual comprehension at this level discussion becomes impossible. When there is consensus about such assumptions they are usually left implicit. When there is no such agreement – and we are far from it in film criticism – self-consciousness about the critical process becomes essential. Not that there is a formula solution to the problem of judging movies. The exploration of theories of film (*models* and *aesthetics*) is not designed to provide a universal and ultimate standard for judging quality; as Pauline Kael says, such 'objective standards' would make the critic unnecessary. And even if they were possible, which they are not, they would

2.   Alan Lovell, 'Robin Wood – A Dissenting View', *Screen*, 10, 2, March/April, 1969.
     Robin Wood, 'Ghostly Paradigm and H.C.F.: An Answer to Alan Lovell', *Screen*, 10, 3, May/June, 1969.
     Alan Lovell, 'The Common Pursuit of True Judgment', *Screen*, 11, 4/5, 1970.
     John C. Murray and Ted Welch, 'Robin Wood and the Structural Critics', *Screen*, 12, 3, Summer, 1971.

make life very boring. Looking at theories of film, rather, is meant to help us in understanding film itself and, just as important, in understanding why people — including ourselves — think some films better than others.

In short, this book will be concerned with the systematic theoretical element in both film *models* and film *aesthetics*. Whether the intention is to develop knowledge or evaluation (or frequently both) it is axiomatic that consistency is important. Without it, argument is no longer practicable; there is more than one debate in film criticism which stems from rapidly shifting and inconsistent assumptions. In my discussion of particular thinkers one of my aims will thus be to explore the consistency of the arguments they invoke. It would be unnecessary to labour this point if it were true that such a criterion was commonly accepted; however, Pauline Kael, in a much quoted paragraph, has clearly missed the point. In her discussion of the 'auteur theory' she asserts: 'It requires more care, more orderliness to be a pluralist than to apply a single theory.'[3] She could hardly be more mistaken. To apply a single theory, of whatever sort, is self-confessedly to attempt to be consistent. To be a pluralist, as Miss Kael suggests, is to pick and choose, '... the best [!] standards and principles from various systems of ideas'. To be flexible, to bend with whatever wind is necessary, to leave consistency behind in the systems from which we borrow. To continue to look at films in the *ad hoc* fashion with which we are so familiar. This book is dedicated to the belief that such an approach is the last thing we want to preserve. Whatever the faults of theoretical self-consciousness, and there *are* some, it does at least create a situation in which communication is possible and in which positions can be argued, expounded, or reformulated. As we have seen, it is impossible to argue with Miss Kael, and above all theory is about argument.

---

3. Pauline Kael, *I Lost it at the Movies*, Jonathan Cape, London, 1966, p. 308.

The Development of Film Theory
Ultimately it would be useful to examine the range of assumptions underlying all sorts of variations in critical practice. This, however, is not intended here. My specific choice of theories and theorists is dictated by two considerations: an attempt to present a sketch of what I take to be the crucial elements in the history of film theory, and an attempt to organize these elements in an analytical context. In both cases the jumping-off point lies in the work of Eisenstein. His remains the one major attempt to coordinate a wide range of knowledge into a full-scale theoretical framework, an attempt which is only now being recognized for what it is. In a sense much of this book, and much of film theory, is concerned with arguments which served to push Eisenstein's contribution into the background. His work was frequently drawn on as a justification for certain *aesthetic* postures, and its importance *in toto* was thus largely ignored, misrepresented, and misunderstood. The standard image of Eisenstein as an arch-priest of *montage* cinema involves, at the very least, a misplaced emphasis, but an emphasis which proved controversial enough to direct attention away from Eisenstein's true interests.

To appreciate the consequences of this for film theory, we must trace the development of a particular cluster of primarily *aesthetic* themes. In the practical beginnings of film we find the roots of what was to follow. Film developed from photography, and, to the nineteenth-century thinkers, the characterizing achievement of photography lay in its ability to reproduce reality. The most efficacious of the highly valued realist painters could not hope to compare. So when the Lumière brothers made those first brief films, their subjects, not unnaturally, came from their immediate physical environment. The train, the baby, and the gardener with his hosepipe. But with almost indecent haste the new invention also found a place with Georges Méliès, a magician who saw in film the new fount of illusion. For him, monsters, planets, and space-travel. The

17

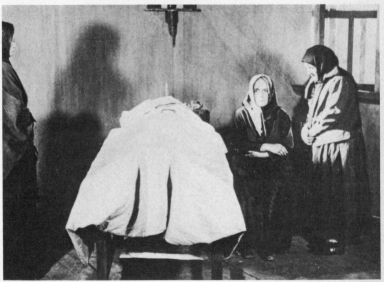

The 'art' of film: *The Cabinet of Dr. Caligari* (Robert Wiene); *Mother* (Pudovkin)

18

shoots growing from these seeds were to split film *aesthetics* in two; the symbolic opposition between Lumière and Méliès hovers perpetually over *aesthetic* debate.

The crucial polarity, then, became that between, on the one hand, realism, naturalism, and the minimum interference of the film-maker, and on the other hand, fantasy, expressionism, and the formative influence of the film-maker. Which is not to say that realism versus fantasy is identical to naturalism versus expressionism; it was merely made to seem that way. One of the earliest interests of film *aesthetics* – the attempt to establish that film could indeed be justly called Art – was deeply involved in this division. The silent films which were claimed as 'artistic' were those in which the 'creative' interference of the artist was most evident. The painting-influenced designs and 'serious' subjects of German Expressionism were invoked as evidence, as were the newly developed *montage* techniques of the Russians. *Caligari*, *Potemkin* and *Mother* were used to define the 'art' of film. Another source of artistic respectability lay in the extravagant Freudian symbolism of the French *avant-garde*. Films like *Un Chien Andalou*, *The Seashell and the Clergyman* and *Ménilmontant* were used to demonstrate that the cinema could be just as experimental as its artistic neighbours. By the time the silent era reached its culmination aesthetic orthodoxy took the part of what Kracauer calls the 'formative tendency'. In the generic imagery, Méliès was on top! And worse still, a bowdlerized version of Eisenstein became an accepted Old Testament.

Eisenstein's major interest was in the workings of film 'language', and he conceived *montage* as a crucial element in such a process. But as we shall see his notion of *montage* was by no means simple, and certainly never as simple as the version held by the aesthetic orthodoxy. His analysis was complex to a degree, requiring and making a number of conditioning assumptions. The social and psychological contexts in which the cinema operated were the primary focus of these assumptions.

Lumière: *A Boat Entering Harbour*

In the former case Eisenstein's views were fairly straight Soviet socialism; in the latter, a Pavlovian behaviourism. Either way, this context was left largely undiscussed within the Eisenstein canon. It is in later and otherwise unimportant side-tracks from the main development, in particular the works of John Grierson and Rudolf Arnheim, that the context problems were re-raised. As far as the mainstream of aesthetic development was concerned Eisenstein *seemed* irretrievably associated with the 'Film as Art' school of the silent period. When this tradition proved unable to cope with the coming of sound (unlike Eisenstein himself), his much more interesting theories sank with the rest. The pendulum swung toward Lumière. The documentarists of the 1920s, Renoir in the 1930s, and Italian neo-realism in the immediate post-war years, were a progression of 'realism'. The aftermath of war produced a cinema

Progressive realism: Renoir's *La Marseillaise*

properly fitted to a realist *aesthetic*: the less the artist interfered with the reality before his camera the better the film. Eisenstein, a realist in some respects, could now be definitely proscribed as a formalist (in this, at least, Stalinism had beaten the new aesthetics some years earlier), and his *models* of film were consistently interpreted as *aesthetic* dictates. First André Bazin, and then Siegfried Kracauer, produced elaborate 'justifications' for the resurgence of a realist cinema. The horns of the dilemma were firmly fixed. Although compromise always remained possible in principle, practice always seemed to involve realism *or* formalism, non-interference *or* interference, Lumière *or* Méliès. For a while film theory became obsessed.

The general form of this 'realism deadlock' has underlain a number of aesthetic debates. The argument over the coming of sound, for instance. Sound, seen by the traditionalists as the

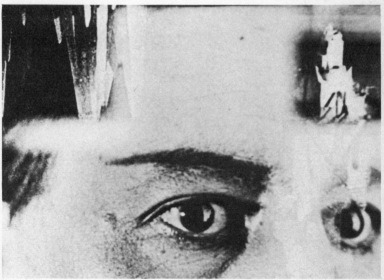

Un Chien Andalou (top); *The Sea-Shell and the Clergyman*

22

great destroyer of an established visual art, was held up by the new aesthetics as an asset to realism. And even when the formalist schools finally accepted that sound was here to stay they preferred to focus their interest on the 'creative use of sound'. Traditionalist textbooks to this day retain chapters thus labelled. And in much more recent years we have seen established an opposition between the 'natural' and uncluttered American cinema and the 'aesthetic' and more complex European cinema. The net result of such absolutist divisions has been to press film theory into the ready-made moulds of realism versus formalism, and to effectively prevent anything but sterile polemic. In the end the only way of escaping the polarity is to retreat entirely from the strictly *aesthetic* discussion on to the more neutral ground of methodology. Recent years have produced just such a development, a change in focus from problems of evaluation to problems of descriptive interpretation.

The pattern of this 'historical' account should indicate my interests. It seems to me that Eisenstein's work has become overlaid with many years of *aesthetic* argument. Although he by no means solves them, Eisenstein does raise, explicitly or by default, a series of analytically crucial problems in the theory of film. He attempts a beginning analysis of film language, his work clearly demonstrates the need for a more extensive discussion of the social and psychological context of film, he is the interstitial figure in the realism debate, a debate which in turn has pushed film theory back toward the problems of method to which Eisenstein partly addressed himself. It is with these problems that this account of film theory will primarily be concerned.

Not surprisingly then, the first body of theory I shall discuss is that proffered by Eisenstein himself. Chapter Two is entirely devoted to an attempt to draw together some of the disparate elements in his many essays. Two sets of problems grow out of this. First, the problem of context, both social and psycho-

23

logical. I shall *briefly* raise the question in Chapter Three in relation to the work of John Grierson. Second, the realism issue, most notably the arguments advanced by Bazin and Kracauer. If Eisenstein is a pillar of film theory, these two are clear candidates as *aesthetic* door-posts. Chapter Four will be devoted to them. Chapter Five will be concerned with the 'retreat' from *aesthetic* theory and the beginning interest in the methodology of film criticism. In particular, the theory of *genre* and the so-called 'auteur theory'. And finally, in Chapter Six I shall try to suggest the possible direction of development of film theory.

Clearly what follows is a small selection from a large body of film theory, and sometimes a highly critical account. Even within the work of particular authors I have chosen to discuss certain things and not others. Bazin, for instance, had much wider interests than the argument for realism, while my account of Grierson by-passes much of his educational thought. I make no apology for this selectivity. My interest lies in the bits and pieces of film theory and not the whole sweep of ideas on film. I am writing at a time when there seems to be a very considerable interest in the cinema, and when the art itself has undergone some not unimportant changes. We are invited to re-think the traditional postures of film theory, and, like Thomas in *Blow Up*, we are perpetually reminded that there are many ways of looking at the 'real' world. There is always an invitation at such times to dismiss apparently discredited intellectual ancestors as no longer relevant, to start with a clean sheet. However critical I may become in the pages that follow I do believe that it would be to our loss were we totally to dismiss the writers I shall consider here. We have much to learn from both their qualities and their faults.

2: Eisenstein: Great Beginnings

Of the classic writers on film Eisenstein is clearly the most complex. Meyerhold, Freud, Pavlov, the Kabuki theatre, the Commedia dell'Arte, flow in and out of his essays, bound together, more or less, by ill-digested lumps of orthodox historical materialism. Often not orthodox enough, however, and at least some of the stranger leaps in his thought can be accounted for in terms of political pressures. For whatever else he may have been, Eisenstein's thought was far too wide-ranging to be constrained by Stalin's mock philosophy or even Engels' universal and mechanical dialectic. His conception of the relation of film to 'reality' went beyond the simplified world of 'socialist realism'. His was the existence of the goat that hungers for the grass beyond the end of its tether. In both writings and films he was continually pulled back, sometimes by others, sometimes, it seems, by himself. *Bezhin Meadow* and the second part of *Ivan the Terrible* suffered drastically in consequence, while the nationalistic and highly regarded *Alexander Nevsky* is hardly his greatest work. That other famous 'response to just criticism', Shostakovitch's Fifth Symphony, is at least a resounding artistic success!

Much of the problem, for us as well as for the Stalinist establishment, is rooted in Eisenstein's unwillingness to base all

25

aesthetic judgements on one dominant criterion. In an essay which brought about the closure of the journal in which it appeared, he put it bluntly:

A high social appraisal must not serve as a shield, behind which with impunity can be concealed poor editing or a low quality of enunciating those words which, in any final accounting of a film, also determine its value.[1]

In spite of this, however, it does seem that Eisenstein remained a deeply committed socialist for most of his life. The 'romantic' Bolshevism of *Battleship Potemkin* may well be representative. His differences with the State arose from his view of how the aims of socialist film were to be implemented. 'Socialist realism' assumed that audiences would automatically respond to the correct socialist subject matter, leading to, in the end, pedestrian treatment of scenes from Soviet life. Eisenstein took the view that audience responses were rather more complex than this; that film could be used in such a way as to *inspire* an audience with socialist ideas. Through 'pathos', through a unity of form and content, through the formal language of film-making, it was possible to create a more efficacious means of communication. The distinction is rather like that between the speaking styles of the stereotyped university lecturer and the fiery orator; between the wishy-washy romantic realism of *Ballad of a Soldier* (so beloved by Western liberals of the early 1960s), and the equally romantic but immensely more powerful *Potemkin*; ultimately, between a mechanical and formula Marxist aesthetic and a creative but heterodox Marxist aesthetic.

But the political issues are the background to the tasks of this essay. They simply make it rather difficult to answer some of the questions we might sensibly raise about Eisenstein's film theories. For instance, what are we to make of his declining concern with dialectics? Was it simply that his version was too

---

1.   Sergei Eisenstein, *Film Essays*, Dobson, London, 1968, p. 152.

26

'idealistic' for the bowdlerized philosophy and aesthetics of his period, or was he ultimately convinced that 'dialectical' analysis was theoretically insufficient? To further complicate the issue, considerable materials remain, as yet, untranslated from the Russian. In particular, we must eagerly await translations of the unfinished drafts of *Montage, Direction*, and *Art of Mise en scène*. Even so, we can discern four main trends in Eisenstein's thought from the essays available to us. First, a moral commitment to socialism and to socialist aesthetics of one form or another. Secondly, an analysis of the fundamental formal elements of film and the manner of their relation: in the main his approach to the 'language' of film through the concept of *montage*. This is centrally concerned with the 'cells' of cinematic expression and their interaction. Thirdly, a series of ideas about what sort of cinema this language should be used to create, discussed principally in relation to 'intellectual cinema' and *pathos*. Lastly, and underlying the previous two, there is Eisenstein's attempt to root his theories in an eclectic set of anthropological and psychological assumptions as to the nature of man. In this essay I shall be particularly concerned to discuss the second and third of these trends, invoking the first and last where it seems useful to do so.

Dialectics of Film

Although a loose idea of montage appears quite early, more systematic analysis begins in the 1929 essay, 'A Dialectical Approach to Film Form'.[2] Here, Eisenstein argues for a parallel between the method of thought termed 'dialectical materialism', which arises from the 'projection of the dialectical system of things into the brain', and art, which arises from the projection of the same dialectical system of things into the creative process. Artistic creation develops from the interaction of contradictory opposites; the dialectical process (thesis–antithesis–synthesis) is the baseline on which the theory of

---

2.   Sergei Eisenstein, *Film Form*, Dobson, London, 1951, pp. 45–63.

27

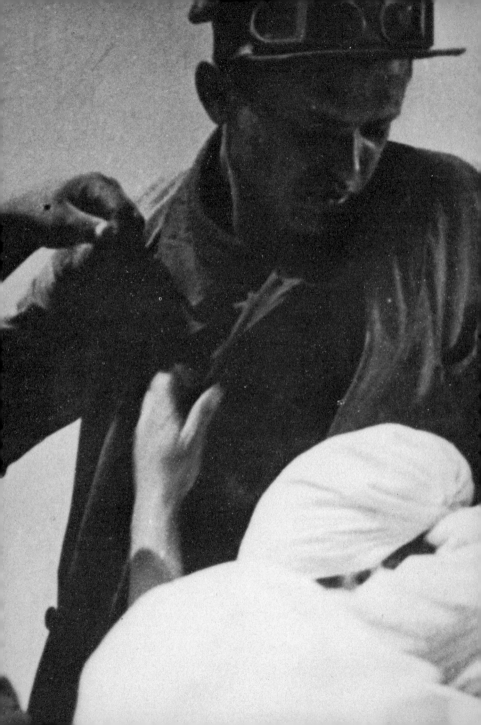

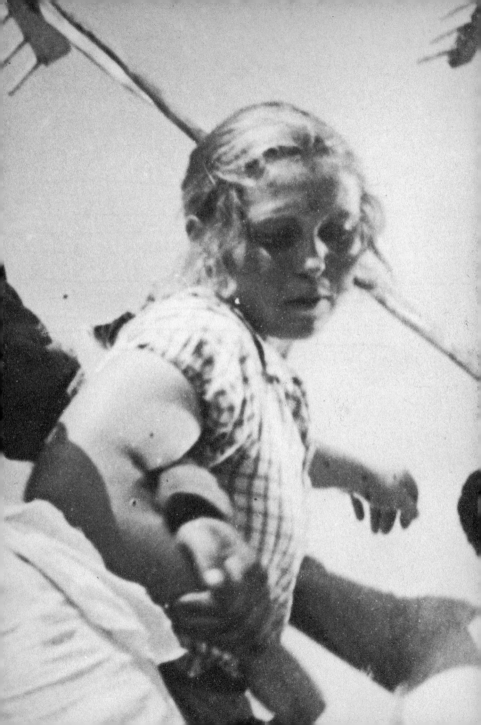

montage rests. The fundamental assumption is that all things in the world are related in a dialectical manner, and so this 'universal' dialectic must find its place in film as much as anywhere else. It is this rather extravagant claim that first marks Eisenstein off from the other Soviet film directors. There is, at least at first, a considerable pressure apparent in his work to use the mould of 'dialectics' to hold his thoughts, accompanied by an equally obvious tendency for them to overflow the sides of the container.

There is a clear sense in which the dialectic provides a rationale for Eisenstein's particular interpretation of the Kuleshov experiments. One, in particular, seemed important to Eisenstein, although the whole set developed a similar theme. By splicing a strip of film showing a shot of Moszhukhin's expressionless face to various other shots in turn (a bowl of soup, a coffin, etc.) and then showing the results to an audience, the experimentors succeeded in showing that the audience believed the face to be expressing the appropriate emotion (e.g. hunger, sadness, etc.) in each case. From this, it followed that one of the important factors influencing an audience's response to a film revolves around the *juxtaposition* of the shots involved. In a word, *montage*. Now, thus far in film history editing had been primarily dictated according to the narrative needs of the film. A cut, when it came, was necessary to move on to the next camera set-up. Only Griffith, most notably in *Intolerance*, had begun to explore the immense formal possibilities of editing, so to the Russians the Kuleshov discovery had all the marks of a fundamental insight.

Characteristically, Eisenstein took it to its most extreme limits. Where Pudovkin, ever pragmatic, saw montage as a process of 'building', of laying 'bricks' end-to-end, Eisenstein tried to conceive it in a theoretically more sophisticated way. For him it was from the 'collision' of independent shots that the meaning arose in the minds of the audience. Now there is one clear respect, which later proves to be important, in which

Battleship Potemkin; Ballad of a Soldier

31

Eisenstein's version is correct. The Kuleshov experiments certainly suggest that a juxtaposition leads to something *new* in the mind of the audience. It is not built brick by brick. We do not have a conception of a face which is then modified by the following shot; rather, we respond to the two shots *as a whole*. The whole is different to the sum of the parts, this much can be allowed to Eisenstein. But the rest of his conception is problematic. Faced with the axiom that the basic elements of film are the *shot* and the *montage* through which the various shots are related, it remains to discover the exact manner of this relation; to find the rules according to which the cinematic language operates. In 1929 Eisenstein's first approximation is in terms of dialectics − the creative 'collision' of opposites. But such an identity of montage and dialectic is a narrow conception indeed, and Eisenstein always seems willing to admit rather less narrowly defined forms. By 1938 the retrospective version of the crucial early days' concept of montage no longer involves 'collision'. Instead, it is '. . . that two film pieces of any kind, placed together, inevitably combine into a new concept, a new quality, arising out of that juxtaposition'.[3] Indeed, *The Film Sense* is devoid of any mention of the dialectic.

This is not a purely scholastic point. Eisenstein's desire, for whatever reason, to employ dialectical conceptions has all sorts of consequences. It leads to a stress on 'conflict' montage in his earlier theoretical writings, a stress which drastically curtails the applicability of the montage idea. Interestingly, once Eisenstein embarks on his more detailed analyses of particular films and sequences many of the 'dialectically' imposed constraints disappear. The 1929 essay may have as its title 'A Dialectical Approach to Film Form', but the approach, if approach it be, barely survives the essay. Eisenstein soon turns to more rewarding pursuits.

---

3. Sergei Eisenstein, *The Film Sense*, Faber, London, 1943, p. 14.

Aspects of Montage

Eisenstein initially distinguishes five types, or bases, of montage: metric, rhythmic, tonal, overtonal, and intellectual. All may exist simultaneously in any given film sequence. I shall consider each in turn. *Metric* montage revolves around the mechanical 'beat' of the cutting. The crucial basis for editing lies in the *absolute lengths* of the strips of film, regardless of what they portray. The strips are in constant proportionate relations to one another. They may be shortened to increase tension, but the proportionate relation is maintained. This is the simplest method of all. Endless early film chases (and some not so early) build up to their climax through accelerating metric montage, and it is clear that Eisenstein sees metric montage *by itself* as somewhat less than worthy. Pudovkin, he suggests in a sideswipe, is the major exponent of the method. The second type, *rhythmic* montage, takes into account part of the visual content of the shots involved; in particular, the pattern of movement within a shot. Eisenstein himself is initially much concerned with the possibility of conflict between the metric and the rhythmic types. Hence his own example from the Odessa Steps sequence of *Potemkin*. The soldiers' feet as they descend the steps set up a rhythm *within* the frame which is not synchronized with the metric beat of the cutting. Thus the film builds tension through the simple metric method and also through violating that method at key points. Equally, however, it is possible for the two methods to reinforce one another. Otsep's *A Living Corpse* (a neglected classic of the 'extreme' montage period) contains a very impressive gypsy dance sequence where metric and rhythmic bases are mutually reinforcing. The more frenetic the dancing movement within the frame, the faster the metric montage. Similarly with many of the passages in Ruttmann's *Berlin*.

These two aspects of the montage pattern – I hesitate to call them different methods since they are so often intertwined – are very much part of modern editing stock-in-trade. In most films

Madigan (Don Siegel)

34

which treat editing as anything more than something necessary to facilitate the narrative, they can easily be found. *The Wild Bunch*, as I shall suggest in more detail later, is full of such cases. The 'Blue Danube' sequence in *2001: A Space Odyssey*, the pattern of footsteps in the long echoing corridors of *Point Blank*, the climactic sequence of *Masque of the Red Death*, and the tour-de-force at the end of *Madigan*, also offer cases. They are the fundamentals of *tempo* in a work. And pursuing this metaphor, Eisenstein's third type, *tonal* montage, has rather more to do with melody.

Tonal montage is a little more complex. Eisenstein distinguishes it from the rhythmic case in the following way:

In rhythmic montage it is movement within the frame that impels the montage movement from frame to frame. Such movements within the frame may be of objects in motion, or of the spectator's eye directed along the lines of some immobile object.

In tonal montage, movement is perceived in a wider sense. The concept of movement embraces *all effects* of the montage piece. Here montage is based on the characteristic *emotional sound* of the piece — of its dominant. The general *tone* of the piece.[4]

The emotional sound, he continues, can be assessed accurately. For the emotional conception 'more gloomy' we can find a suitable 'light tonality', a suitable degree of illumination. For a 'shrill sound' we can find a relevant visual pattern of angles to provide 'graphic tonality'. And, of course, in Eisenstein's later work we also find considerable interest in colour tones. He again uses *Potemkin* as an example. The 'fog sequence' montage is based on tone. The pieces are assembled on the basis of their light quality ('haze' and 'luminosity'). This is the basic tonal dominant. Beneath this we can also find a rhythmic dominant based on the tiny movements of the ships, the slight movement of the water. In this way, the visual characteristics of the shots set up the gentle, expectant mood of the sequence, which is reinforced by the very slight in-frame rhythmic distur-

---

4.   Sergei Eisenstein, *Film Form*, *op. cit.*, p. 75.

bances. One must be careful, however, in succumbing to the persuasiveness of Eisenstein's example. Although there is evidently a case for singling out this form of montage it is insufficiently specified. Even accepting that it has only to do with plastic formal properties of the shot (that is, nothing to do with particular narrative content), the sorts of rules of relations between emotional and visual tones implied by the analysis are not available even now. Thus, although such a category may usefully direct our attention in the course of specific analysis, to reach the level of Eisenstein's ambition requires a much greater psychological knowledge, or a number of dangerously extravagant assumptions. This latter is Eisenstein's strategy.

There are even more problems with *overtonal* montage, Eisenstein's 'filmic fourth dimension'. Again the idea is developed via the musical analogy, the montage being built on the basis of the total stimuli offered by a shot rather than on particular dominants. One includes in the montage rationale the *overtones* and *undertones* of the shots. The basis for this form of montage is somehow the *totality* of impression offered by each shot, and it was on the editing table, Eisenstein claims, that he discovered *post hoc* that what he had already edited of *The General Line* did not fit into the orthodox categories he had developed. In the 'creative ecstasy' of making the montage he had edited the film on the basis of the whole range of stimuli provided by the shots. It was only when the shots were seen in movement that the new stimuli, the 'overtones', emerged. For this reason examples are problematic:

. . . it [the visual overtone] cannot be traced in the static frame, just as it cannot be traced in the musical score . . . overtonal conflicts, foreseen but unwritten in the score, cannot emerge without the dialectic process of the passage of the film through the projection apparatus, or that of the performance by a symphony orchestra.[5]

Even given this ambiguity, overtonal montage is far from clear.

---

5. Sergei Eisenstein, *Film Form, op. cit.*, p. 69.

Is it really a similar sort of category to metric, rhythmic and tonal? Or is it simply that the first three categories are ways of breaking down the montage effects, while the latter attempts to capture its overall characteristics? Eisenstein is not too clear, but I would incline to the latter interpretation. Overtonal montage is simply another way of talking about montage based on the total effect of the piece; metric, rhythmic and tonal are categories for analysing this process.

These four, or three, whichever the case may be, have both physiological and emotional effects. Eisenstein implicitly suggests whole series of hypotheses about their physical and emotional consequences. But he is also concerned with the possibility of formal montage characteristics having intellectual consequences; with the possibility of *intellectual montage*. The classic examples in Eisenstein's films, albeit simple ones, are always taken from *October*. One commonly invoked case is the sequence in which a series of images of various religious idols are cut together, moving from the most modern Christian representations to the most primitive native figure. The intent is to pull back '. . . the concept of God to its origins, forcing the spectator to perceive this "progress" intellectually'.[6] A further obvious, and crude, example is the famous 'Kerensky climbing the steps' sequence in *October*. The shots of him climbing are intercut with titles ascending the scale of military rank and with a mechanical peacock preening itself, the intention being to make a direct intellectual point.

There are all sorts of problems associated with this classification, some of which I have already touched on. It is, for instance, debatable as to whether *overtonal* factors can be treated in the same way as the others. Such a conception seems to encompass the whole range of response of an audience to a film which, of course, is exactly what we are trying to analyse through the various sub-categories of montage. We have no way of capturing total response without employing some set of

6.   Sergei Eisenstein, *Film Form*, *op. cit.*, p. 82.

categories such as the three basic montage types. Overtonal would thus become a redundant category, or at best a somewhat ambiguous half-idea. Extensive problems also exist with 'intellectual' montage, finding their expression in some rather peculiar psychological assumptions. Thus the alleged lack of qualitative difference between intellectual and other forms of montage is based on the fact that

... there is no difference in principle between the motion of a man rocking under the influence of elementary metric montage [this refers to a sequence in *The General Line* which induced some members of the audience to rock from side to side with the metric pattern] and the intellectual process within it, for the intellectual process is the same agitation, but in the dominion of the higher nerve centres.[7]

Apart from any other consideration this omits the question of the different effects which culture may have on intellectual as opposed to physical response. Even if it is not totally incorrect, it is a much too simplistic conception, related basically to the particular brand of Pavlovian behaviourism espoused by Eisenstein. Inevitably these simpler ideas yield to the deepening knowledge of the years.

Changing Ideas

Ten years sees the main development of these changes. His crucial essay 'Word and Image' (also known as 'Montage in 1938') begins significantly:

There was a period in Soviet cinema when montage was proclaimed 'everything'. Now we are at the close of a period during which montage has been regarded as 'nothing'. Regarding montage *neither as nothing nor everything*, I consider it opportune at this juncture to recall that montage is just as indispensable *a component feature* of film production as any other element of film effectiveness.[8] (my italics).

The reader could be forgiven for thinking that it was Eisenstein

---

7. Sergei Eisenstein, *Film Form*, op. cit., p. 82.
8. Sergei Eisenstein, *The Film Sense*, op. cit., p. 13.

himself who once proclaimed montage everything, and that conceiving it as a 'component feature' (rather than 'the nerve of the cinema') is not something he might reasonably *recall*. Still, such deviousness is intelligible when we remember that Eisenstein was defending himself, as ever in these years, against the frequent charges of formalism. What better way than to deny that he ever elevated the formal aspects of montage to solitary dominion? One should, he now admits explicitly, give equal attention to both formal characteristics of film (montage) and to content. His earlier works were specific researches into one aspect of the whole; they should not be taken as anything else. The aim now is to elaborate the principles whereby the particular representations of each shot relate to the general theme. Unfortunately, he never isolates these principles or what he elsewhere refers to as the 'laws' of such a process. It is this above all which makes *The Film Sense* an ultimately unsatisfactory thesis.

Meanwhile, the concept of montage itself undergoes the generalization implicit in the altered position. In response to the critic who might ask (and who probably did) what the performance of an actor on a single uncut piece of film has to do with montage, Eisenstein now replies − everything! We must look for montage *within* the actor's performance. Now, the conception of film acting that accompanied Eisenstein's montage theory of the 1920s was *typage*: crudely, a playing down of the importance of acting and as a corollary the use of 'types'. 'Actors' were used as elements in the frame but moulded by the director through montage. The point was made in the editing. But with a more general montage conception more orthodox acting is permissible. Or perhaps if acting *must* be made permissible *then* montage will have to be generalized. Either way, as with Hitchcock, Eisenstein still seems to retain a view of actors as 'cattle'. The physical contortions required of Cherkassov in *Ivan the Terrible* exemplify the extent to which he was more interested in the plastic properties of his actors

39

Молнин

than in their histrionic talents. Nevertheless, the *theory* undergoes a generalization and montage becomes, effectively, a way of formulating the relations of parts to wholes. A stage actor, for example, creates his persona out of many detailed elements; together they make up the character. A director creates a theme through all the various *partial representations* of it. The modified view can be expressed thus:

Before the inner vision, before the perception of the creator, hovers a given image, emotionally embodying his theme. The task that confronts him is to transform this image into a few basic *partial representations* which, in their combination and juxtaposition, shall invoke in the consciousness and feelings of the spectator, reader, or auditor, that same initial general image which originally hovered before the creative artist.[9]

Instead of a particular 'dialectical' theory of the role of certain forms of editing in film, the montage concept is now employed to encompass a much wider range. All the multiform elements that make up a film can be conceptualized within the new scheme. At its bluntest the axiom is that parts make up wholes, and wholes are rather different from the sum of their parts. Out of this grows the idea of *vertical montage* – the general process of realizing an effect through relating two separate parts of the cinematic whole. The paradigm case for Eisenstein is in the relation between sound 'pictures' and visuals, initially developed in *Alexander Nevsky* and extended to include colour in reference to *Ivan the Terrible*.

This phase of Eisenstein's writings provides a great deal of fascinating detailed analysis of examples (throughout *The Film Sense*) though relatively little completed theorizing. In many ways the later essays are less specifically theories of film, and more 'notes toward' a general conception of artistic experience. At one level we find Eisenstein elaborating a set of very general ideas about part-whole relations, the notion of synecdoche, and

9.   Sergei Eisenstein, *The Film Sense, op. cit.,* p. 33.

some scattered linguistic parallels. At another level, stimulating accounts of particular sequences which do not bear a clear relation to the more general formulations. Evidently his frequent references to 'structural laws of process and rhythm' and 'laws governing the construction of the form and composition of art-works'[10] imply that such laws are the crucial mediating factors. We can gratefully echo the sentiment, but nowhere does Eisenstein offer a clear statement of these 'structural laws'. Certainly the direction of his later work seems potentially lucrative involving, as it does, the attempt to establish a general method of analysing a whole range of 'languages'. Only the execution, perhaps understandably, remains wanting.

There is, of course, a further set of questions which I have not yet properly touched upon. Much of Eisenstein's concern is with the problems of analysing the *formal* language of the medium. The questions he spends most time on have to do with the effects of the formal ways by which the parts of cinema may be related. Montage, in both specific and general conceptions, is involved with such issues. But there are also questions about what sort of wholes these parts should make. What sort of cinema should be created? These are the questions to which I shall now turn.

What Sort of Cinema?

Eisenstein's approach to such questions most often arose in response to the repeated accusations of 'formalism'. Although he remained very much committed to a Soviet socialist cinema, to 'the liberation of the consciousness from all that representational structure linked to the bourgeoisie',[11] he was frequently in conflict with the Soviet establishment as to how such an aim should be properly achieved. The earliest of his heterodox conceptions was 'intellectual cinema'. A cinema whose prime aim was the communication of ideas: 'a concrete sensual trans-

---

10.   Sergei Eisenstein, *The Film Sense, op. cit.*, p. 128, and *Film Form, op. cit.*, p. 130.
11.   Sergei Eisenstein, *Film Essays, op. cit.*, p. 98.

lation to the screen of the essential dialectics in our ideological debates. Without recourse to story, plot, or the living man'.[12] In the 1929 essay from which these lines are taken, 'Perspectives', the idea is advanced with evangelical fervour. This, for Eisenstein, was a fitting innovation in the realm of film to match the greater innovation of the new proletarian society. A cinema which *directly* imparted its intellectual content.

Inevitably there were pressures against such a view. It was, they said, formalistic; it did not truly concern itself with the masses. One might be tempted to add now, with that eternal advantage of hindsight, that Eisenstein never really suggested how to attain such a cinema anyway. However, he yielded, and his writings suggest a mixture of genuine mellowing and outside pressures. In his speech to the All-Union Creative Conference of Workers in Soviet Cinematography in 1935, he had this to say about the theory of 'intellectual cinema':

This theory set before it the task of 'restoring emotional fullness to the intellectual process'. This theory engrossed itself as follows, in transmuting to screen form the abstract concept, the course and halt of concepts and ideas − without intermediary. Without recourse to story, or invented plot, in fact directly − by means of the image-composed elements as filmed. This theory was a broad, perhaps even a too broad, generalisation of a series of possibilities of expression placed at our disposal by the methods of montage and its combinations. The theory of intellectual cinema represented, as it were, a limit, the *reductio ad paradox* of that hypertrophy of the montage concept with which film aesthetics were permeated during the emergence of Soviet silent cinematography as a whole and my own work in particular.[13]

He then goes on to argue that the crucial 'dialectic' (the term is now almost empty) in art is that involving both thematic-logical thought and sensual thought. To place undue stress on one or the other, as the intellectual cinema would stress the themato-

12. Sergei Eisenstein, *Film Essays*, *op. cit.*, p. 46.
13. Sergei Eisenstein, *Film Form*, *op. cit.*, p. 125.

Kino-fist: *Strike* (Eisenstein)

logical, is to fail. It is the unity of these forms of thought which produces a true work of art.

The notion of unity is now increasingly prominent. Montage is still important but *within the context of, and unified with, the other elements of film*. Hence, in 'The Structure of the Film', the weight of discussion revolves round 'organic-ness' and 'pathos' in particular relation to *Potemkin*. A work is organic, argues Eisenstein, where the *laws* by which the work is created correspond to '... the law of structure in natural organic phenomena'.[14] The nature of this law remains unfortunately obscure, although Eisenstein's passing reference to Engels' *Dialectics of Nature* once more suggests the possibility of the universal application of the dialectic. As ever in his later work, Eisenstein sheers away and we are left with the familiar gap

14.   Sergei Eisenstein, *Film Form*, *op. cit.*, p. 160.

45

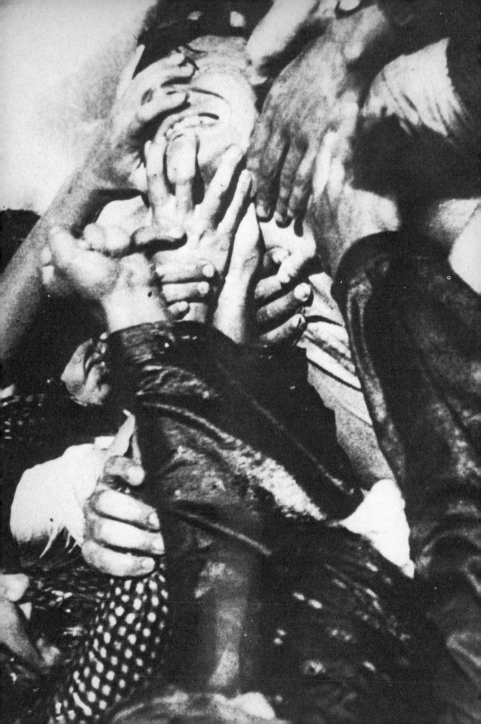

between general statement and detailed analysis. There are similar problems with 'pathos', the process whereby a spectator is lifted 'out of himself', electrified, raised into ecstasy. How to reach such intensity is again only partly clear, although Eisenstein makes much of the parallel between montage techniques and the pattern of the creative process.

The strength of montage resides in this, that it includes in the creative process the emotions and mind of the spectator. The spectator is compelled to proceed along the selfsame creative road that the author travelled in creating the image.[15]

One element, then, is in the shared creative ecstasy produced through the montage process. The spectator is also artist. But, as a cursory look at his films would suggest, Eisenstein was also very much aware that this formal element was not the whole story. Other factors would needs be invoked. What does remain clear, however, is that 'pathos' is very much the *aim* of Eisenstein's cinema. The goal is, in his unfortunate terminology, to create the 'pathetic' film!

This militant, fiery, pathos style, this 'kino-fist', is the style, Eisenstein says, of *Strike*, *Potemkin*, *Mother*, and *Arsenal*. It arises from the social militancy of the revolution and, in the later case of *Alexander Nevsky*, from the fervour of Soviet nationalism. But 'kino-fist' is not all, and Eisenstein is forced to remark, in passing, a rather more prosaic means of attaining 'pathos'. This 'quieter' method is epitomized in the *Maxim Gorki* trilogy, but it is clear that Eisenstein's sympathies lie elsewhere. In the end they can be traced back to the Pavlovian reflex psychology with which all of Eisenstein's thought is permeated. Given the correct set of stimuli, there then follows the correct 'pathetic' response. Modify this slightly with the notion of *organic unity* (loosely formulated) of the elements of film, and we know why *Potemkin* is experienced as intensely moving all over the world. Even, Eisenstein suggests, the class

---

15.   Sergei Eisenstein, *The Film Sense*, *op. cit.*, p. 34.

Kino-fist: *Strike*

Prosaic pathos: *The Childhood of Maxim Gorki* (Donskoi)

enemy can be so moved. Behind the anthropological discussions, the arguments about modes of thought, there is the belief that the montage techniques somehow resonate with something fundamental to man's nature regardless of the cultural clothes in which he is dressed. Ultimately Eisenstein takes a mechanistic view of human nature. From this comes the proposition that the unspecified laws of thought give rise to the equally unspecified laws of cinematic structure. Perhaps the odd references to Engels are more than a simple justification in the Marxist–Leninist canon.

It would, nevertheless, be difficult to deny that Eisenstein the film-maker was extraordinarily successful in exploiting the capacities of the medium for 'pathos'. And equally, those formal factors which he does single out as important in creating 'kino-fist' are not to be neglected. The problem is to avoid some of the dressing in which the salad rests, and then to add something more than radishes. It is because of these confusions, the imbalances of his ideas, and some of the barren psychological and sociological assumptions with which he was operating, that his work is not great theory. Is it, however, a great beginning to the process of theorizing about film?

Great Beginnings?

One way of answering this question is to ask how his work can be of use to us today. We have become accustomed to the idea of Eisenstein as the arch-prophet of editing, particularly the techniques of contrast and irony developed in *October*. For criticism and appreciation of film this provides a useful viewpoint on *one formal* aspect of the medium. For the rest, the argument might go, we must look elsewhere. This is evidently only partly true, as Eisenstein was himself aware. The charge of creating, in *montage*, a monistic criterion for assessing a film is an unfortunate exaggeration. His views on criticism were rather less extreme. Thus, in his essay 'A Close-Up View' he draws an analogy between the use of long shot, medium shot, and close-up in film making and three aspects of film criticism. A film can, and should, be looked at in these three ways. The 'long shot' which is concerned to explore the ideological (or moral) correctness of a film. The 'medium shot', the view of the normal spectator and primarily concerned with the 'living play of emotions'. Finally, the 'close-up', which is concerned to break down the film, analyse its parts and the manner of its working. All these are essential elements for the consideration of the critic; no single one can justify accepting a film as good if others are defective. All three approaches must be pursued.

The relation of this scheme to the rest of Eisenstein's theorizing is obvious. The theorizing itself is the 'close-up' technical analysis. The understanding attained in this way is directed toward involving the ordinary spectator in the intense emotion of the 'pathos' structure. Through this involvement 'the general characteristics of the theme enter the spectator's consciousness *en passant*. The generalized concept of the event is embedded in the spectator's feelings.'[16] The spectator grasps thematic content through his emotional response to the film; form and content are united. Eisenstein's tragedy was that the established Stalinist position elevated the form-content distinction to a fundamental law. The ideologically proper position must imbue the whole film; Eisenstein's wish to grip the spectator in an iron fist led to insufficiently obvious ideological rectitude. Reality was there and Eisenstein wanted to mess with it. As we shall presently discuss, that allegation is still being made. But it is to his credit that he did not try to elevate some master belief to the level of sole arbiter of aesthetic taste. Sometimes, in his more polemical discussions of montage, he hovered near to it, but always the position was finally rescued. His thinking at least has the virtue of flexibility.

Still, other than as 'advice to young critics', what use is Eisenstein's work? The answer I think can take two forms. One involves a long-term investment in the ultimate usefulness of his views of the language of film, the creation of pathos, vertical montage and the rest, as a partial basis for a more thoroughgoing theory of film. The other has to do with using his thought in the course of our analysis of particular films as and when it proves useful. Clearly our understanding of the formal montage elements of film can be facilitated by using Eisenstein's views at least as signposts. The more a film (or sequence) depends on montage techniques, then the more useful the theories. Some directors, Howard Hawks, John Ford, Michelangelo Antonioni, for instance, make virtually no use of classic montage techniques. Since we are not elevating Eisenstein's ideas into a system of aesthetic values this implies nothing about the quality of their work. Others, Alfred Hitchcock, Don Siegel, Sam Peckinpah, are variously dependent on montage for some elements of their cinema. This has

16.   Sergei Eisenstein, *Film Essays*, *op. cit.*, p. 151.

no consequences for the intensity of any 'pathos' that may result: both Ford and Peckinpah can be as intensely moving as any directors I know, using very different techniques. Indeed, Peckinpah seems to me to be above all the modern montage director, at least in his two *epic* films – the tattered *Major Dundee* and *The Wild Bunch*. Let me illustrate some uses of Eisenstein's work in exploring the formal determinants of the intense effects of the final reel of *The Wild Bunch*.

The sequence I have in mind begins with Pike and the Gorch brothers in the brothel. At this point the montage is solely concerned to carry the simple narrative. There is no clear metric or rhythmic pattern; the pace and visual tones are gentle and subdued. This combines with two thematic references to elsewhere in the film: the solitary guitar recalls Angel's playing at an earlier camp, while the Mexican girl and her child locate Pike firmly in the 'might have been' world of his past love. This poignancy is reinforced in the formal technique, the 'vertical montage' between music and visual tonality. The mood hangs and flutters like the briefly intercut bird on a string. Finally it is broken, aurally and visually, by the first synchronized words of the scene. For the last time comes Pike's ritual 'Let's go!'; 'Why not?' is the reply. Again the intercut bird, now panting on its back. Like the ants and scorpions at the beginning, like the peacock in *October*, this is a typically Eisensteinian imagistic comment. The peaceful intermezzo is over; the bird is in its final throes.

Collecting Dutch, they move to their horses. In narrative terms we are still unaware of what they intend. But as they form up and arm, in what irresistibly look like pre-determined positions, the wide screen is suddenly dominated by the pattern of the four men in a row. They set off to rescue Angel and there follows a *tour de force*. Every montage technique is involved at one level or another. The basic tempo is laid down by the metric cutting pattern, accelerating slightly as the sequence progresses. This is the baseline of growing tension. Overlaid on

51

this is the rhythmic montage, cutting on the basis of movement within the frame. Here there is mutual reinforcement between the 'stepping out' of the four men (like the soldiers on the steps in *Potemkin* and, incidentally, in many of the angles involved, like the march to the corral in *Gunfight at the OK Corral*) and the beat of the metric montage. From front or back four-shots of the Bunch filling the screen the cut is either to side-angled two-shots (one very notable one of Pike and Dutch) of head and shoulders moving irresistibly on, or to various *static* groups of Mapache's troops. This supplies a rhythmic montage contrast between Bunch and troops, much as a similar technique did with troops and populace on the Odessa Steps. Tension is built and everything carries us with the Bunch. They become gargantuan. On top of this is added the tonal montage pattern, on the basis of the clean visual line of the Bunch and the messy, chaotic scatter of the troops. To match the visual pattern, the troops are shot in a sort of dust-haze while the Bunch remain optically clear. Thus the basic tempo and 'melody' montage techniques screw us to an increasingly high emotional pitch.

Over this basic pattern Peckinpah adds further elements of vertical montage: in particular, the music. This is a combination of the guitar and voices of the villager's farewell song and the rhythmic side-drum first heard in the build up to the opening massacre. In tempo it matches the metric and rhythmic montage, thus providing a perfect combination of visual and aural patterns, and its volume increases as the tension grows. But the music itself is also based on a montage conflict. The drum recalls the massacre while the song evokes the beauty of the departure from the village. Embedded in it is the thematic joining of the extreme violence of the Bunch to the romantic and idyllic appeal of the village. The music thus performs the double function of supporting both the formal intensification of 'pathos' *and* the thematic development that, for the first time, the Bunch is involved for 'altruistic' reasons. Through the total

The death of Angel

emotional involvement comes the theme, much as Eisenstein
envisaged in his discussions of 'pathos'.

At the climactic point all tempi cease. The four men once
more fill the screen. Everything hangs suspended because the
rhythm, resonating across several levels of the film, has been
cut off. In the ensuing exchange the metric pace again suddenly
accelerates at the point of Angel and Mapache's death. Again a
long, held shot, smiles of relief, Pike raises his pistol and shoots
the German. All hell breaks loose. What follows is principally
comprised of very rapid metric montage, the pattern of which
competes with the frequently slow-motion movement within
frame; a metric-rhythmic conflict. Occasionally the tempo is
completely broken to single out particular points: Pike's
'Bitch!' to the girl who shoots him; the Gorch brothers dying
endlessly in slow motion; Dutch and Pike exchanging looks

Breaks in the tempo: the girl shoots Pike; and (right) the Gorch brothers dying

behind the table. The impossible frenzy is finally stopped as Pike and Dutch sink down to their deaths.

The fourth 'movement' begins in unearthly silence with, once more, simple narrative montage. Shots are mostly long; only Thornton's quiet removal of Pike's gun is in close-up. In typically Eisenstein fashion Peckinpah cannot resist inter-cutting the bounty-hunters with the buzzards. As Thornton seats himself and the 'refugees' stream past him, the weight of formal technique rests with the visual tone. Silhouetted buzzards, mute colours, and dust. The cuts are imperceptible; the pace has been slowed right down. The film fades away, pausing only to recall the Bunch, jumping from Thornton and Sykes to the five dead men on the basis of laughter, and from them to the departure from the village once more. Perhaps this is part of what Eisenstein meant by overtonal montage.

This has only been a brief application of *some* of Eisenstein's ideas relating to particular formal elements in film. The fact that I have not considered, for example, the importance of our already established ambivalent attitude to the Bunch does not mean I am indulging in formalism. The idea is to illustrate the usefulness of some of Eisenstein's ideas on aspects of film 'language', not provide a definitive analysis of the final reel of *The Wild Bunch*. In a loose sense it does seem to me that the ideas are useful. I say 'loose' because at this stage in our understanding of film language all such analysis is bound to be loose. Eisenstein's basic conceptions of montage do provide us, in my view, with a useful starting point for exploring certain elements of cinematic 'linguistics'. Similarly, treated as a particular mode of communication among others, his ideas on 'pathos' are of some interest, particularly in their stress on

Dutch and Pike

communicating theme through emotional involvement. But partly because of the faults of the philosophical and psychological grounding of his thought, it is difficult to see his contribution as the great overarching theory he hoped for. As a theorist of cinema, Eisenstein is a man of brilliant ideas embedded in an inconsistent and confusing background. Perhaps the as yet unpublished works will alter this necessarily provisional conclusion. It would be nice to hope. But even if they do not, it is certain that Eisenstein remains head-and-shoulders above most of those who follow him. His great beginnings have yet to be taken up.

3: The Problem of Context: John Grierson

Eisenstein's great obsession was the language of film. He brought a wide range of learning and a sharp intelligence to bear on this element of cinema. But to focus in such a way on a specific part of film, to look in detail at the 'technical' workings of the medium, required him to operate within a whole range of assumptions. In other words, he assumed a certain context. Take his discussions of *montage* 'rhythm'. It is now a commonplace to assume that accelerated cutting raises the level of emotional tension in an audience. In terms of behaviourist psychology, that the stimulus provided by a particular pattern of rhythm provokes a certain response on the part of the audience. Now much of Eisenstein's analysis of *montage* rests on such ideas of tempo, or, at least, on more complex versions of this basic notion. This sort of suggestion about psychological response to a particular set of stimuli can be one (or both) of two things: either a straight psychological assumption, or part and parcel of a larger psychological body of knowledge. To explore the particular phenomena that interested Eisenstein some such assumption was essential, and in his case he undoubtedly felt it justified in terms of Pavlovian reflex psychology. Of course, if the assumption is demonstrably wrong, or limited in particular ways, then serious questions must needs arise about any theory of film employing it. Assumptions about the psychological context of the cinema are necessary in our theorizing; but for the sake of clarity they must be made specific.

This need for context assumptions holds true for both *models* and *aesthetics*. It is not possible to construct an aesthetic system in a vacuum. At the very least a body of aesthetic standards has some relation to the ways in which their author conceives his world, his social life, and the role played by film in this larger context. Bazin and Kracauer, the 'philosophical realists', attempted to construct an aesthetic system which would be in some part 'context-free'. They tried to ground their criteria of evaluation in what they selected as the basic essence of the medium itself. In effect, they argued that the medium has a natural (and presumably eternal) affinity for particular forms, specifically what Kracauer calls 'the redemption of physical reality'. But of course there is no 'essence' of a medium apart from our perception of it; the medium is not an objectively given and isolated entity. It is part of a physical, psychological, social, and cultural context, and to talk about it at all is to make a set of assumptions about such a context. As we shall see in the next chapter, the characteristic arguments of the 'philosophical realists' are deeply problematic for all sorts of detailed reasons. But a not inconsiderable part of the difficulties they experience stems from the attempt to construct an aesthetic in a vacuum. Their context assumptions remain implicit.

Unless the theorist's task is to be hopelessly complex, however, he must call a halt somewhere. Imagine we are interested in the basic 'language' elements through which a film communicates, as was Eisenstein. To facilitate our analysis we make certain assumptions about the characteristic response to any particular configuration of 'terms' in this language. If an audience sees a character in long shot, from above, and dwarfed by his environment, it will conceive him as weak, isolated, and lonely. This is the standard text-book point usually invoked with reference to the later scenes in Xanadu in *Citizen Kane*.

60

This in turn depends upon a set of psychological assumptions about the ways in which we emotionally respond to particular perceptual situations, and such assumptions are themselves grounded in a body of psychological theory and knowledge. Obviously the theorist of film cannot be expected to turn aside and devote a few years to these more general psychological concerns. He takes them as given and gets on with his particular tasks. Continuing the same example. The theorist may make his psychological assumptions, but they could in turn be conditioned by a further set of, say, sociological assumptions. It might be the case, for example, that in our society people respond to certain perceptual situations in the expected way. But in another society different patterns of social life and social structure alter the particular psychological response. Our theories are then 'culture-bound'. Eisenstein, for example, clearly believed that he had tapped some sort of fundamental 'human nature' in his assumptions about particular sets of stimulus and response. Perhaps he did. And even if he didn't, it might be that his particular assumptions enable us to get good enough results to justify their use as limited approximations. But they do exist, and although the theory of film is not to be *reduced* to a psychology or sociology of film, the theorist must be aware of the point at which he has said 'thus far and no further'.

A corollary of this is that there is some need to explore these contextual factors further, in particular the psychological and sociological. This means more than simply the development of a psychology and sociology of film. It also suggests the need for a less specialized awareness of the role of the social and psychological context in our responses to, and evaluation of, film. This much is clear from Eisenstein's work. Historically, however, the mainstream of film theory left the question there and with few exceptions the generation that followed Eisenstein swallowed his assumptions whole. Film theory was developed as if it were context-free. Until the realist debate came to dominate the field only John Grierson and, to a lesser extent, Rudolf Arnheim took up the problem unknowingly bequeathed them by Eisenstein. Arnheim pursued his interests into areas outside of our present scope and into the more general realms of a psychology of art.[1] Grierson, on the other hand, developed an aesthetic *explicitly* grounded in his more general views of society and the role of the cinema within it. In so doing he became the first major exponent of a socially derived theory of film, a strand of thought which thenceforth continued to weave in and out of the literature.[2] In centring his aesthetic on a morality of social responsibility he elevated one element in the context of film to the pinnacle of aesthetic importance. It is this original claim which still makes him interesting.

Grierson: Purposive Cinema

Grierson's theory, if such it is, was not formulated in the abstract. It was not the fruit of an extended and systematic reflection, but rather a set of loosely related ideas which grew out of his experience in the documentary movement in England, Scotland, and Canada. His writings are perhaps best conceived of as weapons in a lengthy, single-minded, and practical fight for what he saw as a socially responsible branch of the cinema. Thus, in attempting to distil the essence of his

1. See, for example, Rudolf Arnheim, *Film as Art*, Faber and Faber, London, 1958, and, among others, Arnheim, *Art and Visual Perception*, Faber and Faber, London, 1956, and *Towards a Psychology of Art*, Faber and Faber, London, 1966.
2. This 'socially conscious' tradition has been visible in a number of contexts. In the 'commitment' arguments surrounding the position developed by Lindsay Anderson: see, for example, 'British Cinema: The Descending Spiral', *Sequence*, 7, 1949, and the famous 'Stand Up! Stand Up!', *Sight and Sound*, 1956. In the concern with popular culture in its social context: see, for example, Stuart Hall and Paddy Whannel, *The Popular Arts*, Hutchinson, London, 1964. And, finally, in the interesting work of one of the blacklisted writers of the 'red scare' period, John Howard Lawson, *Film: The Creative Process*, Hill and Wang, New York, 1964.

Shanghai Express (Josef von Sternberg)

argument it is always possible to overstress a view which may only have been formulated thus for the immediate purpose of debate. For instance, there is more than one occasion on which Grierson denies that he would wish to extend his arguments specifically in support of documentary to apply to all films; his is the pragmatic acceptance of more than one type of cinema. But there *is* in his work a clear sense of the general desirability of realism — 'fresh air and real people' — and social responsibility, the factors he developed as the keynote to documentary. This belief that the medium should disport itself responsibly, almost weightily, turns up frequently in his general film criticism. Much though he admired the Joe Sternberg of *The Salvation Hunters* and *The Exquisite Sinner*, the 'von' of *Shanghai Express* becomes the maker of an empty film. To Grierson it is '. . . a masterpiece of the toilette', an ineffective disguise for the thinnest of themes. It is Sternberg's fall into vacant aestheticism which prompts the lovely aphorism 'When a director dies, he becomes a photographer.'[3]

The criticism becomes more pointed on the Hitchcock of the 1930s and, incidentally, on the 'aesthetic' critics of the period.

I believe the highbrows, in their praise of him, have sent Hitchcock off in the wrong direction, as they have sent many another: Chaplin, for example. They have picked out his clever little pieces, stressed them and analysed them until they are almost everything in his directorial make up. We have waited patiently for the swing of event (preferably of great event) to come into his films, something that would associate him more profoundly with the dramatic wants of common people. Something serious, I am afraid, will have to happen to Hitchcock before we get it.[4]

'Great events' and the 'common people'. A seriousness of purpose and a sort of populism are the keys which run through

3. Forsyth Hardy (ed.), *Grierson on Documentary*, Collins, London, 1946, p. 38. (The current extended edition is published by Faber and Faber. Page references to the first edition.)
4. *ibid*, p. 51.

Drifters

Grierson's work. Not entirely unleavened with admiration for
the 'aesthetic' touch or with pleasure in the 'froth' of
Hollywood, but these are always secondary to the main concern. Technique must invariably be subjugated to purpose. The
founding film of the documentary movement, *Drifters*, though
obviously stylistically influenced by Eisenstein, ensured that
the style must always be harnessed to the dominant idea.
Grierson is a pragmatist of the people; his first concern is with
society, and the 'art of film' is a rather distant second. In his
own terms the documentary movement 'used' the aesthetes,
Cavalcanti and Flaherty. However great Grierson's admiration
for *Nanook* and *Moana* he remains unhappy with Flaherty's
Rousseauesque and romantic views. In his greatest moments of
evangelical fervour Grierson conceives himself as struggling
against the whole of individualist culture. It is very reluctantly

65

that he admits to still finding '. . . the greatest image in rhetoric is the single man against his horizon, seeking his destiny',[5] an image which comes very close to typifying Flaherty's cinema. Grierson is altogether rather uncomfortable with its incarnation in *Man of Aran*, and although his essays revolve principally round documentary, the arguments he invokes are general enough to spread their wings throughout his writing. In the end his is a case for an *aesthetic* of film, not simply a justification for documentary.

His views on film grow out of his analysis of twentieth century society; he thus has a practical social interest in film theory. For him the cinema has a potentially great role to play in the solution of twentieth century problems. Problems like maintaining peace, increasing international understanding, and maximizing opportunities for citizenship. The justification for one form of film as against another, for realism as opposed to fantasy, for the collective ethic as opposed to the individualistic, lies in this social role. Ultimately Grierson's reference point is democracy with a capital D. Mass media, he argues, can be the binding which will hold our societies together. And the cinema – this is, of course, before the rise of television – is potentially the most powerful among them.

The particular form of his argument derives very much from Lippmann's famous account of the failings of contemporary education and democracy. Change, it runs, is all-pervasive in the twentieth century. Even should he wish it, the individual is no longer able to keep track of the changes, the problems, the issues of his day. But the traditional conception of democracy hinges on the 'informed citizen' as do traditional educational techniques. Education is out of touch with the new demands of these large societies, while the mystical participatory notion of democracy has been left entirely behind by events. What is required of the mass media is that they cover all sectors of society in order that these various social elements can remain

---

5.   Forsyth Hardy (ed.), *Grierson on Documentary*, p. 198.

Housing Problems

in contact with one another. They should serve to reinforce ideas of citizenship and of collective destiny. Like *Drifters*, *Night Mail* and *Industrial Britain*, films should increase our awareness of the range of the new world and the magnitude of change. Through such awareness, Grierson assumes, we will come to understand our world the better. Like *Housing Problems* and *Workers and Jobs*, film should venture directly into social problems and social criticism. They should show '.... the common man, not in the romance of his calling as in the earlier documentaries, but in the more complex and

Industrial Britain; Housing Problems

68

intimate drama of his citizenship.'[6] And at the most general level of all, the cinema should shift its focus from '... the drama of personal habits and personal achievements' to the collective and cooperative element in modern life. Within societies and across the world man must be unified. Film, says Grierson, '... is the medium of all media born to express the living nature of interdependency.'[7]

This, then, is the argument of a reformer. Thirty years later it sounds at the very least a little romantic. What looked like a great and powerful medium then, now looks to be a relatively minor instrument of persuasion. 'Democracy' seems rather less of a worry, at least in Grierson's sense, and it is clear that simply to show the rest of the world in their normal pursuits does not have the automatic benefits which Grierson tended to assume. In many respects his argument has dated, as would any case derived from specific social conditions, and Grierson was above all a social pragmatist. Unlike the 'philosophical' realists who try to justify realism in less socially sensitive terms, he is rarely to be found considering the 'medium' *per se*. Rarely does he invoke photography, and its affinity to reality, as the fount of cinema, and then only in passing. For him the intention was clear, the *raison d'être* practical, the method realistic. If film was expensive and the moguls unsympathetic (he frequently raises this as *the* obstacle to a good cinema), then turn to the Government, turn to the sponsors. If the 'big films' are inaccessible, then the little documentaries will do. If aesthetic choices must be made then Grierson's path is clear: realism.

The penalty of realism is that it is about reality and has to bother for ever not about being 'beautiful' but about being right ... In our world it is especially necessary these days to guard against the aesthetic argument. It is plausible and apt to get under the defences of any maker in any medium. But, of course, it is the dear bright-eyed old enemy and by this time we know it very well. Documentary was

6. Forsyth Hardy (ed.), *Grierson on Documentary*, pp. 148–9.
7. *ibid.*, p. 247.

from the beginning — when we first separated our public purpose theories from those of Flaherty — an 'anti-aesthetic' movement.[8]

Grierson asks that the cinema come to earth. Although his argument for realism over and against aestheticism is made in the context of the documentary movement, it must clearly apply to the whole range of cinema. If he seriously wished to achieve his social aim then the whole cinematic castle must be captured, not just the outposts. He asks that the cinema should keep in touch with the 'common people', and is saddened by this failure in the later films of Eisenstein, Pudovkin and Dovzhenko. *The General Line*, *Deserter* and *Earth*, he says, suffer in that their directors are alien to the material with which they are working. Interestingly it is the neglected Ermler — occasionally remembered for the montage ingenuity of *Fragment of an Empire* — whom Grierson singles out from the Russians. The truth is that Grierson's populism derives not a little of its power from a deep-seated mistrust of 'highbrows' in particular, and the middle-class in general. As we have already seen, Hitchcock was allegedly undone by the highbrows. In a more evangelical strain Grierson is concerned for Cagney:

It [the cinema] began in the gutter and still trails the clouds of glory with which its vulgar origin was invested. But if we ask it to go deep, be sure we are not just asking it to go middle-class. And be sure that the next phase of cinema may not be to eliminate the Cagneys in favour of the Colmans and indeed to Colmanise Cagney himself.[9]

The implied siding with 'popular' culture as against 'high' is a brave sally in advance of its time and a reflection of Grierson's frequent expression of his cinematic aim as sociological. This last, presumably, in the traditional English sense: what has been aptly called 'a kind of Marxified Fabianism'! Whatever sympathy one might feel for Grierson's position,

8. Forsyth Hardy (ed.), *Grierson on Documentary*, p. 179.
9. *ibid.*, p. 72.

and it would be difficult not to feel any, his *aesthetic* argument is clearly problematic. Even allowing the particular social analysis it is not at all clear why *realism* should follow of necessity. His intention, after all, is not simply to show one half of the world how the other half lives. Although the early years of the movement saw the production of many such films, Grierson came to conceive of them as the weakest weapon in the armoury. More important to him was to enter the arena of social debate, and, ultimately, change people's ways of thought, their cultures. What he is really asking for is a purposive cinema; if you like, a 'moral' cinema. Obviously not in the limited sense, but an attempt to encompass the concept of social responsibility in the cinema, to include the 'moral' dimension in criticism as the overriding concern. But, of course, there is no good reason to suppose that Grierson's realism, its material shot 'in the raw', is any more powerful in its effect than is staged cinema. Propaganda is a far more subtle business than it seemed some thirty years ago. As a justification for realism Grierson's argument does not hold water; his is really a case for 'responsible propaganda'. Propaganda that is 'right'.

At heart Grierson sees film aesthetics as a by-product of historical 'destiny'. Society is far too complex to be unified and stabilized in the old familiar ways. The close-knit community has gone, and industrial democracy is unworkable on the old bases. A new and 'Democratic' culture is to be forged and film is the medium to do it. Not merely through spreading information, though this is part, but by creating a cultural context in which social interdependency is a practical possibility. Once Grierson expands his case beyond the simple spread of knowledge then we find two separate strands to the argument. Both begin with a sociological assumption about the nature of the changes experienced in modern society. In the terms developed by the French sociologist, Emile Durkheim, the passage from mechanical to organic solidarity. The form of solidarity characteristic of modern societies is organic: resting on the complex interdependence of the members of that society. For Grierson — although he did not employ these terms — the problem lies in providing a cultural basis for this organic solidarity; a system of beliefs which will make modern, democratic, industrialized societies work. It is not possible to live by total consensus on all points (Durkheim's mechanical solidarity) any longer, and, as I have suggested, Grierson puts forward two interlinked but separable arguments. The one, which leads to documentary in particular and realism in general, sees the spread of information about the range of differences between man and man as a basis for social solidarity. The weakness of this argument, at least as an exclusive case, is that it approaches the problem of organic solidarity with the weapons of mechanical solidarity. It assumes that a consensus achieved by increasing knowledge of the 'real' world will bind society together. Knowing how the other half lives will enable us to recognize and hold on to our common humanity. This assumption does not seem entirely realistic, unless we also assume that the simple spread of knowledge automatically promotes mutual understanding. The evidence hardly favours such an optimistic view.

Grierson himself was obviously not happy with this as it stood. His later essays implicitly develop the view that the problem is rather more complicated than can be dealt with in these terms. So we find a further case made for 'propaganda'. Information and realism are not sufficient. Our films must *involve* the individual in the process of creating solidarity, in the interdependence of his society, in the 'drama of his citizenship'; in Eisenstein's terms, the need is for 'pathos'. Although we no longer live in a simple society depending on common agreement, there is a level at which we can be 'persuaded' to agree: the level of recognizing our interdependence as transcending our differences. And this, of course, is not a brief for any particular aesthetic limitation such as realism. It is an argument that, whatever the particular form, the crucial factor is its social role *vis-à-vis* this fundamental need for solidarity. In the last analysis Grierson's position leads in the direction of the end (providing a culture to underwrite the workings of modern democratic societies) justifying the means (any form of propaganda directed toward this morally accepted end).

Context Domination

Grierson's theory, then, is context-dominant. It elevates one area of contextual concern above all other factors. Pushed to the limit it can have no implications for our aesthetic judgements of film separate from the social function performed by the film. The measures of aesthetic taste are limited to two: the social responsibility of the film, and its effectiveness in achieving this socially responsible aim. As it stands the Grierson argument is no basis for anything more than this and, as such, it exemplifies the problems which have been attendant upon the few attempts to specifically involve context factors in theories of film. the problem is more acute in *aesthetic* argument: in developing *models* of film there is at least a further arbiter, how well the *models* fit the reality. If they do not, then we may be forced to revise the particular form of our contextual assumptions. But *aesthetic* argument is directed toward the justification of a set of general evaluations on the basis of certain axioms, and some of these latter are invariably contextual assumptions. In Grierson's case the position is extreme in that *aesthetic* judgements about film are not simply conditioned by contextual assumptions about the social and psychological role of cinema, they are dominated. Aesthetics is reduced to morally prescribed social theory. 'Purposive cinema' emphasizes the 'purposive' at the expense of the cinema.

It would be entirely wrong, however, to take this as a reason for avoiding the context issue in *aesthetic* discussion. The attempt to develop a context-free aesthetic — the effective aim of the 'philosophical realists' — is just as problematic as Grierson's context-domination. The problem is to find a balance between evasion and subjugation. Aesthetic argument can be reduced neither to 'essence' nor to social (or psychological) discussion. It may be that it ought to combine both. And equally film *models* are neither created in a vacuum (which implies unstated assumptions) nor can they be *reduced* to a sociology or psychology of film. Whatever our theories they must in some ways be abstractions and simplifications. To attack the issue of context is to begin to specify the precise ways in which they are so. Grierson's theoretical importance lies in the impetus he gives to this endeavour.

4: Aesthetics of Realism: Bazin and Kracauer

As we have seen, the spectre of realism has haunted film aesthetics from the beginning. From the moment Lumière singled out the 'rippling of the leaves' as fundamental to film, realism was marked out for immortality. Eisenstein frequently found his wings clipped by its Stalinist variant, while John Grierson bluntly asserted the aesthetic in the context of his moral and political analysis. The standard texts are never without their statutory reference to the realistic propensities of the cinema. Predictably, however, it is outside the Anglo-Saxon context that the tradition finds its full and 'philosophic' flowering. Disparate in style and opinion, the French critic André Bazin and the émigré German academic Siegfried Kracauer share at least their starting point. Often differing on the direction in which their thought carries them, they are both crucially involved in the attempt to create a non-social aesthetic of the real. Theirs is the pursuit of the Holy Grail.

Basically they share two assumptions. The first of these is that a medium possesses certain distinct characteristics which have specific implications for the nature of communication in the particular medium and for any related system of aesthetics. Hence Kracauer's study, '. . . rests upon the assumption that each medium has a specific nature which invites certain kinds of communications while obstructing others'.[1] The special characteristics of film have to do with photography: for Bazin, 'those categories of *resemblance* which determine the species *photographic* image likewise, then, determine the character of its aesthetic as distinct from that of painting.'[2] In other words, to create a valid system of aesthetic standards we must ground it in the central distinguishing characteristics of the medium in question. For those bothered by relativism in aesthetic standards this offers some relief from the flux of subjective judgements; such a criterion seems independent of particular individuals and yet deeply implicated in the nature of the medium. Aesthetic dispute ceases to be in terms of 'what I like' versus 'what you like'. Now the questions to be asked are: 'Is this film genuinely *cinematic*? Does it fulfil the *proper* potentialities of the medium?' Of course, like all solutions to this problem – if indeed it is a problem – the argument is really only pushed back one stage. Instead of making directly subjective judgements about the quality of the film(s), we now make them about the 'essence' of the medium. From this general evaluation, particular judgements follow. In this sense, then, the attempt is misdirected. A body of aesthetic propositions is no more 'objective' for being based on the central characteristics of the medium, and such a method does not necessarily offer any extra justification for the judgements involved. What is the 'essence' of film to one man may well be the residue to another.

The basic assumption of these arguments, then, is not entirely without its difficulties. A second is even more problematic. Here both Bazin and Kracauer fall into what Pauline Kael calls 'the great, lunatic tradition'. The essence of film, they would argue, lies 'in its power to lay bare the realities',[3] in 'the

1. Siegfried Kracauer, *Theory of Film: The Redemption of Physical Reality*, Oxford University Press, New York, 1965, p. 3.
2. André Bazin, *What is Cinema?*, Vol. 1, University of California Press, Berkeley and Los Angeles, 1967, p. 15.
3. *ibid.*, p. 15.

redemption of physical reality'. There is a natural affinity between the cinema and the recording and revealing of reality, an affinity which becomes the central axiom of the realist aesthetic. The problems raised by this assumption are very extensive and their discussion forms a large proportion of this chapter.

Both writers wish to found all aesthetic judgements on the central characteristics of the medium *as they perceive them*. If, for the sake of making any progress at all, we bracket discussion of this questionable procedure, we can then explore the divergent cases put by Bazin and Kracauer. It is perhaps worth noting at the outset that Bazin seems the more sympathetic of the two, if only because his work is far less deliberately systematic. The reality aesthetic is something that *informs* most of his work, and if he does not seem to sink into the quicksands in which Kracauer flounders, it may only be because he does not push his position to its limits. This has been left to some of his more recent followers. Kracauer, by way of contrast, offers a teutonic epic to match any of the silent German films on which he has so extensively written. One is irresistibly reminded of the well-known sociologist who writes, it has been said, in Heidelberg English. But even if his assumptions are faulty, if some of the argument is blurred, and if the build-up is laboured, Kracauer at least tries to formulate a consistent aesthetic system. The execution may falter but the intention seems legitimate. And because he tries to be systematic, Kracauer, above all, shows us some of the strange places to which the realist aesthetic can lead. What may be implicitly involved in Bazin is desperately explicit in Kracauer. For this reason, even if for no other, it is useful to turn first to *Theory of Film*.

Kracauer: Systematics of the Real
Theory of Film attempts to cover a wide area. It involves two separate arguments in support of the realist aesthetic, and a

79

Musical 'realism'? Fred Astaire and Ginger Rogers in *Top Hat*; and (right) Gene Kelly in *Singin' in the Rain*

sometimes laborious drawing out of the implications of the theory. I do not intend to much concern myself with the inconsistencies and oddities of this last. Pauline Kael's scathing review (most reviews were highly complimentary), 'Is There a Cure for Film Criticism?'[4] provides ample evidence of his specific peculiarities. Perhaps one or two will serve as signposts for the rest. Witness the way in which he squeezes the Musical into the 'goody' category by dint of arguing that Astaire's dancing emerges from the real-life events of his films, though *Top Hat* hardly seems a paragon of realism. And, evidence of the peculiar limits of his discussion, he fails entirely to mention the Gene Kelly of *Anchors Away* and *Singin' in the Rain*, who is probably a far better example in support of his case. Or again, the way in which he rescues *Song of Ceylon* from hell-fire and perdition by arguing that its montage sequence (a sin against realism, though since he likes early Eisenstein perhaps only sometimes a sin) serves to make the 'real' sequences around it that much more real. This ignores the fact that the sequence in question is a way of developing forcefully one of the main themes of the film. Or, lastly, his failure to recognize that the romanticism of *Louisiana Story* is more than 'simply' a moral issue, but can also impinge on the 'realism' of the movie. And so it goes on, with Kracauer turning this way and that apparently in an effort to 'fit in' all his favourite movies. As a practical guard to the gates of cinematic heaven his judgements are odd. To understand why we must turn to the chapter and verse.

Kracauer makes two central arguments in support of his position. One is fundamental to the whole theory; a second is added almost as an afterthought. I shall briefly suggest the second, and then explore the first in some detail. Kracauer's

---

4. Pauline Kael, 'Is there a Cure for Film Criticism? or: Some Unhappy Thoughts on Siegfried Kracauer's *Nature of Film: The Redemption of Physical Reality*', *Sight and Sound*, 31, 2, 1962. Reprinted in Pauline Kael, *I Lost it at the Movies*, Jonathan Cape, London, 1966.

Romantic realism: Flaherty's *Louisiana Story*

justificatory addendum is really simply a question of his fitting his view into the intellectual ethos of the time at which he wrote. It is a pessimistic variant of the 'end-of-ideology' thesis of the late 1950s (usefully compared with Grierson's earlier optimism) and is founded on the view that contemporary society is best characterized by the absence of a set of generally agreed beliefs and values. Man is without the ideological shelter once provided by religion; he is aware of the world only through the abstractions of the technological ethos. 'He touches reality only with the fingertips.'[5] He has a need to once more grasp reality, a need which can be met through the cinema (again, cf. Grierson). A realist aesthetic is therefore in tune with the requirements of the age. The obvious problem with this argument is, of course, that this diagnosis of contemporary

5.   Siegfried Kracauer, *op. cit.*, p. 294.

society is not quite as convincing as it might have been a decade ago. It seems less likely now that the 'golden age' beliefs are giving way to a vacuum, and more likely that the beliefs themselves are changing in some fairly drastic ways. One wonders how Kracauer would have reacted to *Easy Rider.*

Happily, though, diagnosing contemporary society is not at present necessary. It only finds a mention here for the sake of completeness. Rather, I shall look at the core arguments of Kracauer's theory, which fall into five linked parts.

(a) It is the essence of photography to incline toward the straightforward recording and revealing of reality.

(b) Film involves photography.

(c) Although film involves other elements (such as editing and sound), photography '. . . has a legitimate claim to top priority among these elements, for it undeniably is and remains *the decisive factor* in establishing film content . . .'[6]

(d) Therefore, film shares with photography the inclination toward capturing unaltered reality. This is its major characteristic.

(e) Hence, given the assumption about basing aesthetic standards on the fundamental nature of the medium, it follows that realism is the principal criterion of aesthetic value in the cinema. The realistic tendency is at one with the very essence of film.

Of these five propositions only (b) seems completely unquestionable. Film, we must agree, does involve photography, although whether the continuous frame photography of the movie camera is *that* close to the single shots of the still camera is arguable. For present purposes, however, there is no need to become involved in the finer points of the argument. The remaining four propositions provide ample material.

First (a): the nature of photography argument. When it

6.   Siegfried Kracauer, *op. cit.*, p. 27, my italics.

actually comes to the point, Kracauer is not so absolutely on the side of the realist angels as this bald formulation suggests. Although he speaks of following the realistic tendency as a *minimum* requirement of the photographic approach, he is also willing to admit that '... the formative tendency [meaning the interference of man], then, does not have to conflict with the realist tendency. Quite the contrary it may help substantiate and fulfil it – an interaction of which the nineteenth-century [photographic] realists could not possibly be aware.'[7] One's heart must go out to the nineteenth-century realists. For them the self-evident distinguishing characteristic of the new medium was that it revealed the world before the lens in considerable detail and with absolute veracity. Their point of comparison was the realism offered by painting. Rather like Thomas in *Blow Up* they believed in the power of the camera as revealer of the world; unlike Thomas, they were never really required to face the consequences of their position. But surely they were correct on the very issues of which Kracauer says they could not be aware, precisely because they were not aware. If we once claim that the revealing function of the camera *vis-à-vis* some given reality 'out there' is the crucial *essence* of photography, as they did and as does Kracauer (and, for that matter, Bazin), then any formative effect which the photographer may have must be a denial of this *essence*. Ultimately this leads to the situation wherein the human agency must be totally removed – angle, exposure, shutter speed, all randomly determined. *Any* human agency has a formative effect. But once this last is admitted it must also be admitted that the 'reality' with which we are dealing is never independent of human agency. The 'reality' revealed by the camera *must* also depend on the photographer. And that admission denies the absolute basis of the realist position.

Because Kracauer is conscious of this problem (presumably) he introduces a number of caveats concerning the relation

---

7.   Siegfried Kracauer, *op. cit.*, p. 16.

between realistic and formative tendencies. The one quoted above is typical. But it is not possible to hold both to the position that there is an independent 'reality' which it is the *essence* of photography to reveal, *and* to the position that the 'reality' revealed by the camera must also depend on the photographer and, for that matter, the audience. If the latter is the case – as it must be for Kracauer since he is willing to admit the place of the formative tendency as appropriate in certain circumstances (an admission which the nineteenth-century realists would not be foolish enough to make) – then the first position is absurd. This is so because to admit the influence of the photographer assumes that 'reality' varies according to who perceives it and how, while the 'essence' position – characteristically nineteenth century – assumes there is one fixed 'reality' independent of the observer. In consequence, once we allow the photographer to creep in, he necessarily undermines the 'essence'. It then becomes necessary to detail the varying conceptions of 'reality' held by photographer and audience, and to distinguish between photography as realistic in *essence* and photography which is *thought of* as realistic. We *learn* to think of photography as realistic in the sense that we accept a photograph as showing whatever was before the lens at that particular moment. This has nothing to do with some mystical essence of the medium; it is a response we have developed until it has become second nature, which, incidentally, is not found in those cultures hitherto lacking photography.

It is basically because Kracauer believes that it is possible to isolate the *essence* of the medium apart from the way in which people respond to it that he finds himself in this mess. Certainly the classic realists were wrong in that they failed to see that some 'formative tendency' must always be present. If the photographic spirit does lie in the neutral revelation of reality, there can hardly be many truly photographic photographs. If this is Kracauer's 'reality' then there are no films in the world which meet his aesthetic requirements. Since he fills over three hundred pages with discussion of films ranging from *Forty-Second Street* through *Hamlet* to *Paisà* we must charitably assume that his conception is rather less strict than it appears. But then what notion of reality does he employ? There appears to be no single answer. But it is clear, whatever variations he may develop, that he cannot acceptably claim to have isolated The Essence of Photography. Instead he is implicitly asserting the commonplace that a photographer can attempt to render the illusion of reality with the minimum of interference, or he can interfere to different extents, in different ways. The dichotomous tendencies epitomized in Méliès and Lumière now become a question of degree; the opening shot of Kracauer's argument reduces to: 'Photographers can variously interfere with the process of photography.' Proposition (a) and the *essence* of photography are no more.

Proposition (c) asserts that photography has top priority among the elements of film; it is decisive in establishing film content. What Kracauer means by this is not entirely clear. The limiting case – the content of a film must be photographable – is uninteresting in this context. But Kracauer offers no real support for, or specification of, this position apart from his previous arguments about reality. That is, having established (!) that the essence of photography is to record and reveal reality, to propose the centrality of photography in film is to arrive at the essence of the film. But why should we accept any element as having top priority? Film is a combination of many diverse characteristics. To sink the lot beneath the iceberg-tip of photography seems unnecessary and misleading. To fail to justify such a procedure is critically criminal. It is clearly an arguable proposition that the differences between movie and still photography far outweigh the similarities, though perhaps when one is dealing with essences ... But Kracauer does not give the problems a decent airing; the possibility is cursorily dismissed within the first paragraph of Chapter Two. It is not that proposition (c) is necessarily wrong – it is an unsupported

87

assumption for which no grounds are presented for accepting it as right.

Proposition (d) falls for a number of very obvious reasons. Even accepting that photography is the top priority in film, the dilution of the 'nature of photography' arguments leaves us only with the assertion that 'film-makers can variously interfere with the cinematic process'. But even by-passing this objection, other of Kracauer's specific assertions can bear further scrutiny. Some of the emphases in his discussion of the basic nature of the medium have changed in the move from photography to cinema. 'The basic properties [of film] are identical with the properties of photography. Film, in other words, is uniquely equipped to record and reveal physical reality and, *hence, gravitates toward it.*'[8] Because a medium is well equipped to fulfil some task it naturally 'gravitates' in that direction. The general assumption is that media tend to operate in the field for which they are best equipped. If we are to take this at its face value all the many films from Méliès to *Planet of the Apes* which are not in the puritan tradition of realism (including many that Kracauer favours) are not just bad films, they are contrary to the *natural* tendency. They should never have gravitated in this direction at all. Some new laws of nature must be in operation! Since Kracauer can hardly mean this, he must, presumably, mean that films are only *really* films in so far as they record and reveal physical reality. Anything else is simply not a film.

But what exactly is this 'physical reality' to the revelation of which the cinema should be devoted? The answer is fascinating.

Now there are different visible worlds. Take a stage performance or a painting; they too are real and can be perceived. But the only reality we are concerned with is actually existing physical reality – the transitory world we live in. (Physical reality will also be called 'Material reality' or 'physical existence', or 'actuality', or loosely just

---

8.   Siegfried Kracauer, *op. cit.*, p. 28, my italics.

'nature'. Another fitting term might be 'camera-reality'. Finally the term 'life' suggests itself as an alternative expression . . .)[9]

Resisting the obvious temptation to infer that anything which is not a stage performance or a painting constitutes 'reality' (or vice-versa), we are left in the midst of a welter of misnomers. Just savour 'actually existing physical reality'! Anything stuck in front of a camera and photographed must surely be actual, must exist, and must be physically real. Whether we believe it to be a man in a costume or the title figure of *The Creature from the Black Lagoon* matters little in respect of its 'actually existing physical reality'. What Kracauer must be concerned with is not whether it is real, but whether it is really real!

And in this respect, one of his synonyms is quite instructive. The expression 'camera-reality', although Kracauer's usage varies, is suggestive of the reality status lent to a subject by the camera. In other words, the tendency for our belief in the truthfulness of the camera to lend credence to the subject matter of the film. Now this clearly gets into complex psychological and sociological questions which are not at all involved in the *formal* notion of reality with which Kracauer is operating. However, his actual *usage* does get close to this meaning. He is prepared, for instance, to speak of Dreyer's *Joan of Arc* as attempting to transform '. . . the whole of past reality into camera-reality'.[10] Since in this case it is not possible to film real reality, the concept of camera-reality must include the possibility of *re*creating reality in front of the camera. It is a tiny step from here to the *creation* of familiar realities (as in most narrative films), and then to creating unfamiliar realities (as in many 'fantasy' films).

Whatever Kracauer may say in principle, like Bazin, he is, in practice, willing to include films which attempt to create the illusion of reality. It is now a question of appearances rather

9. Siegfried Kracauer, *op. cit.*, pp. 28–9.
10. *ibid.*, p. 80.

Neo-realism: *Umberto D*

than one of essences. Indeed, the reader begins to feel that Kracauer is altering the meaning of 'camera-reality' according to the films he likes, instead of judging the films on the basis of the reality criterion. There are no problems with neo-realism, *Umberto D* or *Paisà*. But he also admires *Potemkin* and *Wild Strawberries*, which are hardly easy. And finally he opens nearly all the flood-gates by accepting the presentation of 'special modes of reality' as legitimate. 'Films,' he says, 'may expose physical reality as it appears to individuals in extreme states of mind.'[11] *Any* individuals? This is the licence to print anything, and what started life as a strict aesthetic criterion is now whittled down to an eclectic hold-all.

Which leads to proposition (e): the aesthetically desirable film is the one which lives up to the basic nature of the medium.

11.   Siegfried Kracauer, *op. cit.*, p. 58.

This approaches grand tautology. If we once accept the proposition that the fundamental character of film lies in its ability to represent and record reality, then the argument that a film which does not fulfil this fundamental character is bad, is one of two things. Either the reality proposition is a *definition* of film and in consequence *all* films are therefore aesthetically desirable, or the reality proposition is an *empirical* statement about the nature of film. Since the first is uninteresting the second must be the case. But if it *is* an empirical statement it must be based on the evidence provided by the body of films, that is, if we look at the body of existent films we will discover that their basic common characteristic is their 'realism'. This is evidently not the case. The third 'alternative' is that Kracauer believes 'realistic' films to be good, and chooses an extraordinarily circuitous way of 'justifying' his position. Ultimately such subjectivism seems to me inevitable and not at all disturbing. To Kracauer it is obviously anathema; hence this elaborate and dubious general argument.

As if in recognition of these problems, Kracauer is perpetually hedging his bets.

Imagine a film which, in keeping with the basic properties, records interesting aspects of physical reality but does so in a technically imperfect manner; perhaps the lighting is awkward or the editing uninspired. Nevertheless, such a film is more specifically a film than one which utilises brilliantly all the cinematic devices and tricks to produce a statement disregarding camera-reality. Yet this should not lead one to underestimate the influence of the technical properties. It will be seen that in certain cases the knowing use of a variety of techniques may endow otherwise non-realistic films with a cinematic flavour.[12]

The reader alert to the style of Kracauer's passing amendments will note that we are now concerned with 'interesting' aspects of reality. To pursue this leads back into the maze from which

12.   Siegfried Kracauer, *op. cit.*, p. 30.

we have just departed, so let us look elsewhere. Although Kracauer repeats that the *dominant* aesthetic standard is the film's reality, he is now prepared to admit that unspecified techniques can add just a soupçon of cinema to an otherwise unacceptable mixture! Presumably, then, techniques can enhance films which are already acceptable on the basis of their realism. In other words, films of reality in which the lighting is *not* awkward and the editing *is* inspired must be best of all. Thus we are not concerned with some 'pure' relation with reality, but basically with the efficiency with which a film can create the *illusion of reality*. To commit the heresy of reducing Kracauer's argument to a phrase: the more convincing a film, the better it is.

The only conclusion to be drawn from all this is that Kracauer's main argument ends up going in every-which-way. The only systematic elaboration of a realist aesthetic of the cinema founders at the start. And in Kracauer's case this is immensely important since he does not have the sure touch of Bazin in his discussion of the films themselves. His main quality is in his argument, and his argument is lacking considerably. One of the many reasons for this failure may be that the attempt itself is misdirected. To found an aesthetic on the 'nature of film' is misconceived whatever the problems arising from identifying 'reality' as the crucial element. Ultimately Kracauer derives from the purest of romantic aesthetics. One of his synonyms for 'reality' is 'nature', and it is unspoiled nature which he wishes film to preserve untouched. Clearly he approves of Rossellini, about whom it is said that he reprimanded his cameraman for removing a white rock from a field of dark rocks in which they were shooting. What right had the cameraman, he asked, to 'improve' on nature? Kracauer responds to film in this way − this is what he likes. It is unfortunate that he felt the need to erect such an immense edifice in justification. He really only wants films to be nearer to what he considers 'real life'.

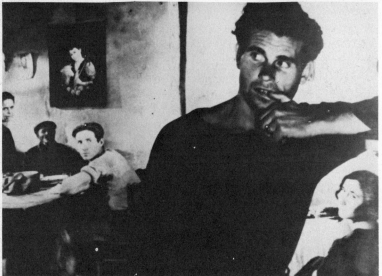

Types of realism: *Farrebique* (top); *La Terra Trema*

97

Bazin: Two Types of Realism

One of the many oddities of *Theory of Film* is its failure to refer to Bazin. Given Kracauer's concern with realist cinema, especially as epitomized in Italian neo-realism, he might reasonably have been expected to draw upon the work of Europe's finest critical authority on the subject. In *Esprit* and *Cahiers du Cinéma* of the late 1940s and 1950s, Bazin wrote extensively on Rossellini, De Sica, Fellini, and the rest. When *Theory of Film* first appeared (1960), two volumes of Bazin's collected essays, *Qu'est-ce que le cinéma?* had already been published.[13] They included in their pages a number of essays relevant to Kracauer's themes, notably 'Ontologie de l'image photographique', 'Montage interdit', and 'L'évolution du langage cinématographique'. This material seems to have escaped Kracauer's attention, a failing for which the theoretical price was rather high. It is not that Bazin escapes the maze in which Kracauer is lost; far from it! It is rather that he displays a sufficiently impressive sensitivity to cinema as to encourage the irrational hope that some of it might have rubbed off on to Kracauer. The combination of Bazin's 'feel' and Kracauer's systematization might just have produced the first (and only) full-scale aesthetic of film. As it is, we have only the two surprisingly independent contributions.

Even so, Bazin does seem to sidle round many of the obstacles into which Kracauer unseeingly blunders. Both authors share a considerable admiration for the achievements of Italian neo-realism; in particular, for the films of Rossellini. And yet Bazin rarely falls into the trap of seeming to formulate a puritan aesthetic which will include neo-realism at the expense of all else. Unlike Kracauer (formally, at least) he admits to different forms of realism. Thus, for example, the distinction

13.   André Bazin, *Qu'est-ce que le Cinéma? I. Ontologie et Langage*, Editions du Cerf, Paris, 1958.
      André Bazin, *Qu'est-ce que le Cinéma? II. Le Cinéma et les autres Arts*, Editions du Cerf, Paris, 1959.

he draws between the 'documentary' realism of *Farrebique* and the 'aesthetic' realism of *Citizen Kane*, both forms allegedly finding their unification in *La Terra Trema*.[14] This willingness to speak of different types of realism can lead to problems in interpreting his position. In *Signs and Meaning in the Cinema*, Wollen takes to task two contemporary inheritors of Bazin's views (Barr and Metz) over their opposition of Rossellini and Eisenstein. The villain for Bazin, he points out, was not Eisenstein, but German Expressionism. But the real problem is that at different times, and in different ways, Bazin occupies both positions. He starts life invoking a case similar to Kracauer's in favour of a 'purist' realism. But this proves too limiting for his much more catholic tastes, and so he also develops a second case for what I shall refer to as *spatial* realism. Unfortunately, he never really brings the two conceptions face to face; never really resolves the strains between them. It seems useful here to take a closer look at these basics of his argument, if only to fully understand how he dodges some of Kracauer's more extravagant disasters.

The 'purist' case finds its main development in the 1945 essay, 'The Ontology of the Photographic Image'. Here Bazin is concerned to isolate 'realism' as the fundamental character of photography and hence of film. He makes a dubious distinction between the two sorts of realism.

... true realism, the need that is to give significant expression to the world both concretely and its essence, and the pseudorealism of a deception aimed at fooling the eye (or for that matter the mind); a pseudorealism content in other words with illusory appearances.[15]

Needless to say, it is 'true realism' of which Bazin approves, although he does not enlarge specifically on what constitutes a 'significant expression'. The distinction is reminiscent of Kracauer's attempt to distinguish what I called the 'really real',

14. André Bazin, *Qu'est-ce que le Cinéma? IV. Une esthétique de la Réalité: Le néo-réalisme*, Editions du Cerf, Paris, 1962, pp. 39–40.
15. André Bazin, *What is Cinema? op. cit.*, p. 12.

and it meets with the same sort of problems. If the 'pseudoreal' fools both eye and mind, then who is to say that it is not truly real? To found an aesthetic on a distinction of this type is rather like founding a morality on the view that murder is only wrong if you get caught. Contrast such a position with that expressed six years later in 'Theatre and Cinema'.

The realism of the cinema follows directly from its photographic nature. Not only does some marvel or some fantastic thing on the screen not undermine the reality of the image, on the contrary, it is its most valid justification. Illusion in the cinema is not based as it is in the theatre on convention tacitly accepted by the general public; rather, contrariwise, it is based on the inalienable realism of that which is shown. All trick work must be perfect in all material respects on the screen. The 'invisible man' must wear pyjamas and smoke a cigarette.[16]

Which implies, surely, that the only reality is the reality of which the audience is convinced; quite conceivably, the pseudorealism which fools the eye and mind. There is a clear contrast between the 'purist' position wherein the cinema taps a fixed 'true' reality and this latter case in which the cinema, by its nature, lends realism to something which is illusory. The most obvious conclusion from the second argument is that the cinema is dedicated to representing '. . . a plausible reality of which the spectator admits the identity with nature as he knows it.' Presumably 'as he knows it' is flexible and depends on a series of social and psychological conditions. Few of us in 1970 'know' the lunar landscape of *2001: A Space Odyssey* in any but the most indirect sense, yet we are willing to accept its realism. But an audience in 1930 would probably have found it much more difficult. In other words, our acceptance of illusion is a *sort* of convention having nothing to do with our metaphysical conceptions about the 'inalienable realism' of the camera.

Clearly there is some strain between the components of the argument. Bazin, an incurable metaphysician, wants to talk of

---

16. André Bazin, *What is Cinema? op. cit.*, p. 108.

Frau im mond

the nature of the medium, its inalienable realism. But his wish to allow 'some fantastic thing' to appear on the screen leads him to the position that something is real if we are fooled into thinking it so. And this depends on a range of factors which have nothing to do with the 'nature' of the medium. Predictably, Bazin expresses unhappiness with the 'plausible reality' explanation. It is over-simplified; insufficiently 'subtle'. Although the failure (to Bazin) of the stagey and implausible décors of *The Cabinet of Dr Caligari* and the rest of German Expressionism lend support to the thesis, there are, he feels, more basic explanations. Like Kracauer, he is unhappy faced with relativism. To make aesthetic judgements on the basis of 'plausibility' raises the familiar bogey: plausible to whom? We are returned (and why not?) to 'I think this is plausible though you do not'. And faced with this, theorists of the persuasion of Bazin and

Kracauer produce the same old response. Back to the funda-mental-nature-of-the-medium argument. Again the comparison between Bazin's 'pure' and 'impure' positions is instructive.

The photographic image is the object itself, the object freed from the conditions of time and space that govern it . . . The aesthetic qualities of photography are to be sought in its power to lay bare the realities. It is not for me to separate off, in the complex fabric of the *objective* world, here a reflection on a damp sidewalk, there the gesture of a child. Only the impassive lens, stripping its object of all those ways of seeing it, those piled up preconceptions, that spiritual dust and grime with which my eyes have covered it, is able to present it in all its virginal purity to my attention . . .[17]

Apart from its extravagant romanticism the most interesting characteristic of this passage is its stress on the *identity* be-tween image and object. Photography impassively reveals the realities of the 'objective' world; it *is* this reality by its very nature. Compare this once more with 'Theatre and Cinema'.

We are prepared to admit that the screen opens on an *artificial world* provided there exists a *common denominator* between the cinemato-graphic image and the world we live in . . . We may say, in fact, . . . that 'the cinematographic image can be emptied of all reality save one – the reality of space'.[18]

'Identity' has become 'common denominator'; 'objective world' has become 'artificial world'. Initially, the fundamental nature of the medium revolves round the absolutes of 'identity' and the 'objective' world. But by 1951 the absolutes have been some-what mitigated. What Bazin is then concerned to discover are the characteristics shared by the 'artificial' world of the film and the world around us. And the most basic of these, he argues, is our normal conception of space. The natural distribu-tion of objects in their spatial context. It is this factor which is then crucial in determining cinematic reality.

---

17.   André Bazin, *What is Cinema? op. cit.*, pp. 14–15, my italics.
18.   *ibid.*, p. 108, my italics.

Rossellini: *Paisà*

These are the basic components of Bazin's two conceptions of realism. Purist realism, at its limit, is the total documentary. It is the neutral, impassive, non-human revealing of an objective world. There is an absolute minimum of interference in the sacrosanct identity of the cinematic image and the object it presents. It is the 'honest' world of Vertov's kino-pravda, of *Nanook of the North*, and, above all, the neo-realism of *Paisà*. The dominant aesthetic criterion lies in a film's faithfulness to outside *natural* reality. Spatial realism, however, derives from a rather different set of assumptions. The objective world, the identity of image and object, no longer figure. Here realism stems from faithfulness to the basic common denominator, the spatially natural distribution of objects. In 'William Wyler ou le janséniste de la mise en scène'[19] we find that Wyler – hardly

19. André Bazin, *Qu'est-ce que le Cinéma? I. Ontologie et Langage*, *op. cit.*, pp. 149–73.

Spatial realism: Wyler's *The Best Years of Our Lives* ▶

The wedding in *The Best Years of Our Lives*

a 'pure' realist – qualifies on the basis of the spatial realism of deep-focus photography. And in his famous essay on realism and the Italian post-war film [20] Bazin develops the contrasting realisms of Welles' *Citizen Kane* and Rossellini's *Paisà*. His hope – partly realized in *La Terra Trema* – was that the two would join.

The problem of these two criteria of realism, in so far as we are concerned with Bazin's thought as a *systematic* aesthetic, is that they are not easily reconciled with one another. Certainly we can say that a good film will be a film which reveals natural reality in a spatially realistic manner. Someone else may then disagree. But the whole tenor of Bazin's approach is to *justify* his aesthetic judgements by reference to the fundamental nature

20. André Bazin, *Qu'est-ce que le Cinéma? IV. Une esthétique de la Réalité: Le néo-réalisme, op. cit.*, pp. 9–37.

of the medium. The difficulty is that he has two fundamental natures, two different views of the same thing. One says image and object are identical; the other that they share a common denominator. One says that film lays bare the objective world; the other an artificial world. If we are really dealing with fundamentals then only one of them can hold. If we are not dealing with fundamentals then they cannot justify any particular type of films as fulfilling the natural potentialities of the medium. Thus, given the misdirected form of argument characteristic of this approach to aesthetics, pure realism and spatial realism cannot both be justified. Like Kracauer, Bazin seems to be unavoidably pushed, against his will, to the extremes. In consequence his practical aesthetic decisions display peculiarities. Were it not for the subtlety of his critical writings, they would, no doubt, look as obviously strange as do Kracauer's.

This can be seen in Bazin's rendering of the realist tradition. Fairly naturally we find him defending Lumière against the incursions of Méliès, though never in crude terms: 'Méliès et son *Voyage dans la lune* n'est pas venu contredire Lumière et son *Entrée du train en gare de la Çiotat*. L'un est inconcevable sans l'autre.'[21] In particular, one suspects, Méliès is inconceivable without Lumière. Continuing on the basis of purist realism the peak of the silent era sees a contrast between the expressionist 'heresy' and the realism of *Potemkin*. The expressionists are so obviously staged, while the Russians are drawing on the natural world. For this, at least, Eisenstein can be hero; *Dr Caligari* is ultimate villain.

But if we now draw in the spatial realism criterion the picture begins to alter. Bazin makes the point in contrasting three products of the German silent era. On the one side *Caligari*, and Lang's *Die Nibelungen*; on the other, Murnau's *Nosferatu*. Presumably, all three must fail on pure realism grounds – the vampire of *Nosferatu* as much as the somnam-

21. André Bazin, *Qu'est-ce que le Cinéma? I. Ontologie et Langage, op. cit.*, p. 27.

Nosferatu

bulist of *Caligari* and the legendary figures of *Die Nibelungen*. But *Nosferatu*, Bazin argues, survives the others (personally, I find them all pretty bad) because it is played out against natural settings, against a world with a common spatial denominator to share with our own. The distorted sets of *Caligari* and the artificial forest of *Die Nibelungen* disobey this basic aesthetic rule. (One wonders how much of this is a spin-off from the 'politique des auteurs'. Bazin, as a great admirer of the later Murnau of *The Last Laugh* and *Sunrise*, may transfer this admiration across the board. *Nosferatu* and the slightly later *Faust* – also played against natural settings if memory serves – seem in the end to be just as much failures as the rest of the German films of the early period.) But in any comparison of the Russian and German silent cinema *Nosferatu*, like the rest of German 'expressionism', would surely come out the loser on grounds of pure realism. There is clearly more than one criterion in play when Bazin lists Stroheim, Flaherty, Murnau and Dreyer as the great carriers of the realist tradition in the silent era.

A consequence of Bazin's switch to spatial realism is that montage becomes the arch-criminal. In the 1930s, Renoir is the sole representative of realism in the cinema:

He alone in his searchings as a director prior to *La règle du jeu* forced himself to look back beyond the resources provided by montage and so uncovered the secret of a film form that would permit everything to be said without chopping the world up into little fragments, that would reveal the hidden meanings in people and things without disturbing the unity natural to them.[22]

Montage, Bazin now argues, is the 'anticinematic process *par excellence*'; proper cinema is to be seen in 'straightforward photographic respect for the unity of space.'[23] Spatial realism thus encompasses his view of both the *plastic* and *language* elements of the medium. Expressionism destroys natural spatial unity by bending it; montage by fragmenting it. Unnatural form becomes the cinematic original sin. What now of *Battleship Potemkin*?

Finally, Bazin sees both forms of realism in the developments of the 1940s. The pure realism of Rossellini and the spatial realism of Welles. But to choose Welles is to enter deep water. Certainly *Citizen Kane* preserves the unity of space through Toland's deep-focus photography. Certainly the cuts are minimized by use of dissolves and joins across the soundtrack. But Welles is, nevertheless, the true inheritor of expressionism (as *The Trial*, *Touch of Evil*, *Macbeth*, and by surmise, *The Third Man*, bear witness), the specialist in the distortion by camera angle, the mysterious shadows once painted but now created through lighting, the grotesque, and the baroque.

---

22. André Bazin, *What is Cinema?*, *op. cit.*, p. 38.
23. *ibid.*, p. 46.

111

The Third Man

Montage and decor are not the only ways of destroying the visual unity of space; almost anything does. Why should they, in particular, be singled out? The immense camera movements of *Touch of Evil* break up the world just as much as montage, and, indeed, serve much the same function in terms of the tempo of the film. If Bazin is really serious about spatial realism a lot more than just montage will have to go. In the end, given that he champions the neo-realists, he must be returned to the argument for pure realism, to the romantic naturalist aesthetic. Peter Wollen puts it well: 'Of *Bicycle Thieves* Bazin wrote that it was the first example of pure cinema. No more actors, no more plot, no more *mise en scène*: the perfect aesthetic illusion of reality. In fact, no more cinema.'[24]

24. Peter Wollen, *Signs and Meaning in the Cinema*, Secker and Warburg/British Film Institute, London, 1969, p. 131.

No More Cinema

If I have spent these many pages attacking the realist aesthetic it is not — as it might have been — because I wish to support a contradictory aestheticism. That debate should be certified dead. Too much time has already been wasted in its by-ways. Both those who take Méliès and those who take Lumière as exemplifying the 'great tradition' are guilty of the same error; an error which Kracauer and Bazin have in common. Refusing the fence of relativism they gallop blindly into the ditch of essentialism. Unwilling to admit the rightful subjectivity of our aesthetic judgements, they dodge the consequent hail of non-problems by recourse to a non-argument. The fundamental character of film, they say, is naturally such-and-such, so any film that fulfils this nature is therefore good. This, hopefully but wrongly, is independent of subjective judgement. Ultimately, both Bazin and Kracauer want a cinema and an aesthetic from which human interference is absent. An immaculate conception!

The tradition is a well-developed one. It reflects above all a romantic faith in nature. Art must passively reveal the natural world. And this faith is very much connected with the equally nineteenth-century conviction that there is some great objective world out there at which we may point our 'artistic' sensibilities. But romantic aesthetics and positivism are not quite the powers that they once were. If we are tempted to reinstate them we would do well to look at Bazin and Kracauer to see where they lead. They lead, as Wollen suggests, to 'no more cinema'. To the paradox that the fundamental essence of film is to destroy everything which distinguishes it as film. And yet Bazin and Kracauer obviously dearly loved a number of films well outside the ambit of their respective pure aesthetics. One can image a fitting epitaph: 'Here lie two theories. Their cinematic eyes were bigger than their aesthetic stomachs, and they perished from indigestion.'

5: Critical Method: Auteur and Genre

As Italian neo-realism declined so also did the importance of the realist aesthetic. In 1960 Kracauer's book saw the last heavy weaponry in the 'philosophical' branch of the tradition. In the related but less complex world of pragmatic realism the moral impetus initiated by John Grierson worked itself out in the 'Commitment Debate' of the late 1950s and early 1960s. This is not to suggest that there are not still skirmishes on either front; the realism issue is far too well installed to simply disappear. But there has been a definite shift away. In some contexts this has led to an increased interest in form, a move toward Eisenstein's area of interest if not toward his terminology. In other contexts the aesthetic question has simply been dropped and the preponderance of effort devoted to an attempt to develop methods of interpretative analysis. Not unnaturally these changes have been related to developments in the cinema itself. In the former case the rise of a 'new' Continental cinema at the end of the 1950s; in the latter an increasing interest in the hitherto neglected body of the American sound film.

It is impossible to assess the magnitude of these changes, but it *is* very clear that the rise in critical estimation of the American film is of vital importance. Not that all critics are now obsessed with American movies. Far from it. The next *Sight and Sound* decade poll will no doubt show the 'intellectual' Continental cinema happily ensconced. But many more

Budd Boetticher's *The Tall T*

people are now prepared to look seriously at a Don Siegel or a Budd Boetticher, with directors like Howard Hawks becoming a good bet for majority respectability where previously only the names of Hitchcock and Ford were whispered – and the latter pretty softly at that! In Sarris' suggestive terms the American cinema has ceased to be the sole domain of the 'forest' critics; there is more inspection of the individual trees.[1] However, it is not the shift itself which is the centre of my attention. The focus here is on what such a shift implies in the realm of film theory. If the realist aesthetic systems and the text-book grammars have gone, what has filled the vacuum they have left? There being no single monumental work on which to base analysis, what can we infer about the theoretical assumptions of much contemporary practice? In short, where, if anywhere, are we headed?

1. Andrew Sarris, *The American Cinema*, Dutton, New York, 1968.

Preminger: *Laura*

The easiest point of entry to such a discussion, lacking a systematized perspective, is through the critical 'language' thrown up by contemporary practice. In particular, through two terms: *auteur* and *genre*. The former has been associated with an amazing variety of positions ranging from the obtusely fascinating to the just plain silly. Some lead to fairly clear aesthetic judgements; others have been more concerned with sympathetic descriptive analysis. Either way the historical root of the term and certain of the assumptions involved are shared. The second term, *genre*, has had a fairly extensive history. For some years it was the principal guideline by which the American 'forest' was mapped. Where Europe had an allegedly free and creative director's cinema, the American, in contrast, was at best seen as a cinema of popular *genre*. Now, however, *genre* has become one of the hinges on which a revived interest in

Walsh: *White Heat*

cinematic language hangs, although it also raises more general questions. In what follows I shall try to partially demonstrate where *auteur* and *genre* may be leading.

Auteur

The most misleading development in contemporary English language writings on film lies in the joining of the two terms 'auteur' and 'theory'. It is something called *the auteur theory* which has provided the touchstone of many a violent dispute. Yet the direct ancestor of the *auteur* usage is to be found in the 'politique des auteurs' of *Cahiers du Cinéma*, in the now famous criticism of Truffaut and his colleagues. How 'policy', the most obvious translation of 'politique', became 'theory' is a tributary in the history of ideas which need not be dealt with here. Sufficient to note that when the *Cahiers* group said

121

'policy' they meant 'policy'. Their use of *auteur* was exactly that: a polemical position marking their views off from the orthodox tradition in French criticism and, ultimately, when they started making films, from the rest of the French cinema. In the England of this period (the early and mid-1950s) opposition to the traditional approach was marshalled under the banners of realism and commitment. Like Grierson before them, these critics mistrusted the commercial American cinema. But in France, fathered though not controlled by Bazin, *Cahiers* used a partisan support of certain American directors against the 'serious' Continental cinema. Which directors exactly varied from critic to critic and group to group, but names like Hitchcock, Ford, Hawks, Ray, Losey, Preminger, and Walsh recurred. It was this polemical and exclusive support for these American figures that was characteristic of the 'politique des auteurs'.

There were thus two notions central to the use of *auteur* from the very beginning. First, the old idea that the director was the true creator of the film. However controversial this may have been in the past (Spottiswoode dedicated his 1935 book to 'the future of the director's cinema')[2] it has surely now passed forever into the realms of acceptability. The old arguments, often tied to the attempt to 'prove' that film was indeed the seventh art, have by and large been successfully arbitrated. While no one would deny the collective nature of film production, the crucial importance of the director's conception is part of the orthodox canon. The Antonionis, the Bergmans, the Godards, and the Fellinis, are accepted as, at the very least, the creative integrators of the disparate elements of film. If *auteur* were simply this then it would have ceased to be controversial years ago. But the second notion involved in the *Cahiers* usage led in a breakaway direction. Applying the notion of director as *auteur* to the maligned commercial

2. Raymond Spottiswoode, *A Grammar of Film*, Faber and Faber, London, 1955.

Hollywood cinema raised a whole new series of bogeymen. In Europe the director was thought to be relatively free from the commercial pressures of Hollywood. It was this 'freedom' which allowed him to be an *auteur*. But for years past conventional wisdom had seen Hollywood as a collection of variously qualified craftsmen turning out variously competent films. Of course, it was never entirely clear that the contrast between the American and European situation was so great; folklore, however, could always fall back on the great artists ruined by the commercial citadel: Stroheim, Murnau, even Eisenstein. What the *Cahiers* critics did was to find *auteurs* where none had been dreamt of before. Directors like Welles, Hitchcock, and to a lesser extent Ford, had always been accorded some admiration. The fate of the émigrés had been bemoaned: Lang, the paradigm case, was frequently and wrongly claimed to have declined in Hollywood. But until *Cahiers* the rest were simply a part of the commercial forest. ART was to be found elsewhere, by definition.

It was this singling out of American directors which was first taken up in the English and American critical context. In America Andrew Sarris provided a focus in the pages of *Film Culture*; in Britain the group of critics writing in *Movie* formulated their own set of American *auteurs*. In both contexts, as indeed in France, there were inevitable extravagances. In employing the notion of *auteur* as a basis for evaluating films there was always the open invitation to elevate the worst films of an *auteur* over the best films of another director *as a matter of course*. Because an *auteur* made the film it must be good. The *reductio ad absurdum* of this position is that it is not necessary to actually see the films, sufficient only to know who directed them. It becomes self-evident that bad Hitchcock (*Topaz*) is better than good Rossen (*The Hustler* or *Lilith*); bad Hawks (*Hatari*) is better than good Zinnemann (*High Noon*); bad Preminger (*Exodus*) is better than good Lumet (*The Hill*). And all of them are better than the 'respectable' European directors.

Zinnemann: *High Noon*; Hawks: *Hatari!*

Ironically enough, it is probably a good measure of the dilettantism of traditional criticism that the Anglo-American *auteur* critics veered so close to these absurdities. For such extreme positions are only really intelligible in terms of the polemical needs of the situations in which they arose. This was guerrilla warfare against an apparently safely established enemy. It was no time for sweet reason.

Hence 'politique des auteurs' led to the formulation of lists, of slogans. The 'Ten Best' ideas were no longer parlour games but declarations of position. The guilty party who added the notion 'theory' to this loosely formulated policy appears to have been Andrew Sarris. In 'Notes on the Auteur Theory in 1962'[3] he provided a rather highly coloured suit of clothes for the polemically naked emperor, and, in addition, an easy opening for attack from the 'traditionalists'. It is only necessary to demonstrate the peculiarities of Sarris' article – hardly difficult – and we can forget about *auteur* forever! The invitation was avidly taken up by that '. . . lady critic with a lively sense of outrage', Pauline Kael, who, carried away on a rising wave of sarcasm, pushed herself into some equally strange corners.[4] She made the still common mistake of throwing out all the *auteur* babies with Sarris' admittedly murky bathwater. Between his theoretical premises and her vituperation most of the point was lost. Sarris, no doubt moved by the salutary experience, made some amends next time round. In a much less extravagant piece he admitted that '. . . the auteur theory is not so much a theory as an attitude,'[5] which is, of course, exactly what it had been up to the Sarris-Kael exchange. Were it not that the rumpus in question is still invoked as the nail in the coffin of the 'auteur theory' (Roy Armes' almost hysterical

3. Andrew Sarris, 'Notes on the Auteur Theory in 1962', *Film Culture*, 27, 1962–3.
4. Pauline Kael, 'Circles and Squares, Joys and Sarris', *I Lost it at the Movies*, Jonathan Cape, London, 1966.
5. Andrew Sarris, *The American Cinema, op. cit.*, p. 30

125

review of Wollen's *Signs and Meaning in the Cinema* is a case in point),[6] it would barely be worth a mention. The fact that it lingers on is a hangover from earlier and more polemical days.

With this debate, if such it can be called, passed the 'auteur *theory*'. In its origins the idea of *auteur* served to isolate the preferences of various groups of critics. It served as a substitute for an aesthetic, a newly developed criterion for making judgements of value. In its pristine form it was obviously unsatisfactory and, pressured by the critical situation in which they found themselves, the *auteur* groups rapidly displayed a tendency to descend into 'aesthetic cults of personality'. Not that this was entirely fruitless. As I have suggested, their great contribution lay in forcing critical opinion to sit up and take notice of the American cinema, hitherto concealed in the fogs of aesthetic obscurity. It is very notable that such established journals as *Sight and Sound*, a decade ago only tossing the occasional snide brickbat in the direction of the *auteur* critics (the '*Cahiers* menagerie' is a phrase that sticks in the mind), now employ the rationale almost as a matter of course. American movies are here to stay, and the genuine polemical days of the auteur aesthetic have probably run their course.

There still remains, however, a considerable 'spin-off', much of which awaits development. The *auteur* position can also be employed as a principle of analysis instead of as a source of critical evaluation. It is the critical *method* to which *auteur* leads that is potentially most rewarding, a point rather missed by the attackers. Pauline Kael:

It's obvious that a director like Don Siegel or Phil Karlson does a better job with what he's got to work with than Peter Glenville, but that doesn't mean that there's any pressing need to go to see every tawdry little gangster picture Siegel or Karlson directs; and perhaps if they tackled more difficult subjects they wouldn't do a better job than Glenville.[7]

6. Roy Armes, 'A Polemic', *Screen*, 10, 6, 1969.
7. Pauline Kael, *op. cit.*, p. 313.

Baby Face Nelson

This passage is very revealing. For one thing it employs the traditional gambit of 'difficult subjects'; this is the snobbery against which the *auteur* critics reacted in the first place, and, interestingly, against which Miss Kael reacts when it shows up in other critics. I am not sufficiently familiar with Karlson but clearly Miss Kael does not look at Siegel or she would never have picked on him. *Invasion of the Body Snatchers*, *Riot in Cell Block 11*, *Baby Face Nelson*, and *Madigan* are hardly simple-minded. It is surely a 'difficult' subject to draw people into the narrative of *Invasion of the Body Snatchers* and also communicate intensely the theme of dehumanization. As Siegel himself says, *Riot in Cell Block 11* resulted in his becoming an 'expert in penology',[8] while *Baby Face Nelson* and *Madigan*

---

8. Alan Lovell, *Don Siegel — American Cinema*, BFI Education Department, London, 1968, p. 8.

offer rather 'difficult' explorations of certain characters within their 'gangster' framework. How does Miss Kael know they are tawdry anyway, if she feels no pressing need to see them? This is the mirror image of the most absurd *auteur* cases: these films must be tawdry because Siegel or Karlson made them. There is some lack in humility here: before dismissing a director's work it is at least reasonable to look at it. *Auteur* used as a method enshrines this from the start. The point is that when we have seen every 'tawdry little gangster picture' they might really turn out to be quite good, precisely because of the insights afforded by looking at the range of a director's work. Whatever else may be said in its favour, through such a process a director as good as Siegel can be rescued from Miss Kael's dustbin.

Alan Lovell puts it well:

By the 'auteur' principle I understand a descriptive method which seeks to establish, not whether a director is a great director, but what the basic structure of a director's work is. The assumption behind this principle is that any director creates his films on the basis of a central structure and that all his films can be seen as variations or developments of it.[9]

The assumption that 'any' director creates on the basis of such a structure is not, however, essential to the working of the principle. It is only necessary to operate 'as if' such an assumption held. If no structure is forthcoming from the analysis then it may be that a director fails to impose his personality on his materials. But we can only discover if this is the case through the operation of the principle in the first place. Hence the 'assumption' is a working hypothesis through which we can make detailed analyses of a director's work. The real assumption of the process is that we can learn more about a director's films by considering them in relation to one another.

---

9. Alan Lovell, 'Robin Wood – A Dissenting View', *Screen*, 10, 2, 1969, pp. 47–8.

There is an obvious way in which this method could be used as a basis for aesthetic judgement. In so far as a director's work does display a central structure then it is good. Equally obviously it would be as well to avoid such a simplistic application. It is a hazardous trail leading back to the extravagances of the earlier *auteur* aesthetics. The more interesting consequence is methodological rather than aesthetic. If the aim is to elaborate the central structure of meaning in a director's work certain analytical facilities are necessary to achieve this aim. The *auteur* principle directs our attention to groups of films having in common one thing – the director. It asks us to isolate his conception of the world as presented in the films, and to do so in some considerable detail. But it does not provide us with the tools necessary for such an analysis. We have a prescription for the direction of our critical action but we still face detailed problems of interpretation. The *auteur* principle is thus a sort of 'pre-theory', a methodological instruction. Whether it is invoked in the analysis of themes, of common stylistic characteristics, or, as Sarris would wish it, in our accounts of film history, it pulls our attention back to film models. For ultimately the sorts of questions suggested by the *auteur* principle can only be answered through detailed and systematic knowledge of the workings of film. To look at films as the work of an *auteur* involves close textual analysis rather than brief critical comment. Unfortunately, we are still not entirely sure of the language in which the text is written. *Auteur* directs our attention back to these concerns.

Genre[10]

Auteur at least originated in film criticism in the recent past; *genre* had a lengthy pedigree in literary criticism long before the advent of the cinema. Hence the meaning and uses of the

10. A longer and slightly different version of this section was published as 'Genre: Theory and Mispractice in Film Criticism', *Screen*, 11, 6, 1970.

The Man Who Shot Liberty Valance

term vary considerably and it is very difficult to identify even a tenuous school of thought on the subject. For years it provided a crudely useful way of delineating the American cinema. The literature abounds with references to the 'Western', the 'Gangster' movie, or the 'Horror' film, all of which are loosely thought of as *genre*. On occasions it becomes almost the end point of the critical process to fit a film into such a category, much as it once made a film 'intelligible' to fit it into, say, the French 'nouvelle vague'. To call a film a 'Western' is thought of as somehow saying something interesting or important about it. To fit it into a class of films about which we presumably have some *general* knowledge. To say a film is a 'Western' is immediately to say that it shares some indefinable 'X' with other films we call 'Westerns'. In addition, it provides us with a body of films to which our film can be usefully compared;

The Last Hurrah

sometimes, the *only* body of films. The most extreme, and clearly ridiculous, application might be to argue that it is *necessarily* more illuminating to compare, say, *The Man Who Shot Liberty Valance* with a Roy Rogers short than with *The Last Hurrah*. Not that the first comparison might not be instructive; merely that it is not necessarily the case. Extreme *genre* imperialism leads in this direction.

Now almost everyone uses terms like 'Western'; the neurotic critic as much as the undisturbed cinemagoer. The difference, and the source of difficulty, lies in the way the critic seeks to use the term. What is normally a thumb-nail classification for everyday purposes is now being asked to carry rather more weight. The fact that there is a special term, *genre*, for these categories suggests that the critic's conception of 'Western' is more complex than is the case in everyday discourse; if not, why the special term? But in quite what way critical usage is more complex is not entirely clear. In some cases it involves the idea that if a film is a 'Western' it somehow draws on a tradition, in particular, on a set of conventions. That is, 'Westerns' have in common certain themes, certain typical actions, certain characteristic mannerisms; to experience a 'Western' is to operate within this previously defined world. Jim Kitses tries to isolate characteristics in this way, by defining *genre* in terms of such attributes: '... a varied and flexible structure, a thematically fertile and ambiguous world of historical material shot through with archetypal elements which are themselves even in flux.'[11] But other usages, such as 'Horror' films, might also mean films displaying certain themes, actions, and so on, or, just as often, films that have in common the *intention* to horrify. Instead of defining the *genre* by attributes it is defined by intentions. Likewise with the distinction between 'Gangster' movies and 'Thrillers'.

Both these uses display serious problems. The second, and for all practical purposes least important, suffers from the notorious difficulties of isolating intentions. In the first and more common case the special *genre* term is frequently entirely redundant. Imagine a definition of a 'Western' as a film set in Western America between 1860 and 1900 and involving as its central theme the contrast between Garden and Desert. Any film fulfilling these requirements is a Western, and a Western is *only* a film fulfilling these requirements. By multiplying such categories it is possible to divide all films into groups, though not necessarily mutually exclusive groups. The usefulness of this (and classification can only be justified by its use) depends on what it is meant to achieve. But what *is* certain is that just as the critic determines the criteria on which the classification is based, so he also determines the name given to the resultant

11. Jim Kitses, *Horizons West*, Thames and Hudson/British Film Institute, 1970, p. 19.

134

groups of films. Our group might just as well be called 'type 1482/9a' as 'Westerns'.

Evidently there are areas in which such individually defined categories might be of some use. A sort of bibliographic classification of the history of film, for instance, or even an abstract exploration of the cyclical recurrence of certain themes. The films would be simply defined in terms of the presence or absence of the themes in question. But this is not the way in which the term is usually employed. On the contrary, most writers tend to assume that there is some body of films we can safely call the 'Western' and then move on to the real work – the analysis of the crucial characteristics of the already recognized *genre*. Hence Kitses' set of thematic antinomies and four sorts of *genre* conventions. Or Bazin's distinction between classic and 'sur-western' assuming, as it does, that there is some independently established essence of the Western which is distilled into *Stagecoach*.[12] These writers, and almost all writers using the term *genre*, are caught in a dilemma. They are *defining* a 'Western' on the basis of analysing a body of films which cannot possibly be said to be 'Westerns' until after the analysis. If Kitses' themes and conventions are the *defining* characteristic of the 'Western' then this is the previously discussed case of arbitrary definition – the category becomes redundant. But these themes and conventions are arrived at by analysing films *already distinguished from other films by virtue of being 'Westerns'*. To take a *genre* such as a 'Western', analyse it, and list its principle characteristics, is to beg the question that we must first isolate the body of films which are 'Westerns'. But they can only be isolated on the basis of the 'principal characteristics' which can only be discovered *from the films themselves* after they have been isolated. That is, we are caught in a circle which first requires that the films are

---

12. André Bazin, 'Evolution du Western', *Cahiers du Cinéma*, December, 1955, reprinted in *Qu'est-ce que le Cinéma? III. Cinéma et Sociologie*, Editions du Cerf, Paris, 1961.

Stagecoach

136

137

isolated, for which purposes a criterion is necessary, but the criterion is, in turn, meant to emerge from the empirically established common characteristics of the films. This 'empiricist dilemma' has two solutions. One is to classify films according to *a priori* chosen criteria depending on the critical purpose. This leads back to the earlier position in which the special *genre* term is redundant. The second is to lean on a common cultural consensus as to what constitutes a 'Western', and then go on to analyse it in detail.

This latter is clearly the root of most uses of *genre*. It is this usage that leads to, for example, the notion of *conventions* in a *genre*. The 'Western', it is said, has certain crucial established conventions – ritualistic gun-fights, black/white clothing corresponding to good/bad distinctions, revenge themes, certain patterns of clothing, typed villains, and many, many more. The best evidence for the widespread recognition of these conventions is to be found in those films which pointedly set out to invoke them. *Shane*, for example, plays very much on the stereotyped imagery contrasting the stooping, black-clad, sallow, be-gloved Palance with the tall (by dint of careful camera angles), straight, white buckskinned, fair, white-horsed Ladd. The power of this imagery is such that the sequence in which Shane rides to the showdown elevates him to a classically heroic posture. The point is reinforced by comparing Stevens' visualization of his characters with the very different descriptions offered in Schaefer's novel. The film 'converts' the images to its own conventional language. Other obvious examples are provided by the series of Italian Westerns. The use of Lee Van Cleef in leading roles depends very much on the *image* he has come to occupy over two decades of bit-part villains. Actors in the series – Van Cleef, Eastwood, Wallach, Jack Elam, Woody Strode, Henry Fonda, Charles Bronson – perpetually verge on self-parody. The most peculiar of the films – *Once Upon a Time in the West* – is a fairy-tale collection of Western conventions, verging on self-parody, and culminating in what must be the most extended face-off ever filmed. Indeed, the most telling suggestions as to the importance of conventions are to be found in the gentle parodies of *Cat Ballou, Support Your Local Sherriff,* and *The Good Guys and the Bad Guys.* Without clear, shared conceptions of what is to be expected from a 'Western' such humour is not possible. One of the best sequences in *Cat Ballou* encapsulates the importance of the imagery, the sequence in which Lee Marvin is changed from drunken wreck to classic gunfighter. Starting very humorously with Marvin struggling into a corset, the transformation not only alters him but brings out a response in us as piece by piece the stereotyped image appears.

In short, to talk about the 'Western' is (arbitrary definitions apart) to appeal to a common set of meanings in our culture. From a very early age most of us have built up a picture of a 'Western'. We feel that we know a 'Western' when we see one, though the edges may be rather blurred. Thus in calling a film a 'Western' the critic is implying more than the simple statement, 'This film is a member of a class of films ("Westerns") having in common x, y, z'. He is also suggesting that such a film would be universally recognized as such in our culture. In other words, the crucial factors which distinguished a *genre* are not *only* characteristics inherent to the films themselves; they also depend on the particular culture within which we are operating. And unless there is world consensus on the subject (which is an empirical question) there is no basis for assuming that a 'Western' will be conceived in the same way in every culture. The way in which the *genre* term is applied can quite conceivably vary from case to case. *Genre* notions – except the special case of arbitrary definition – are not critic's classifications made for special purposes; they are sets of cultural conventions. *Genre* is what we collectively believe it to be.

It is for precisely this reason that *genre* notions are so potentially interesting. But more for the exploration of the psychological and sociological interplay between film-maker,

139

Cat Ballou

film, and audience, than for the immediate purposes of film criticism. (Given that it is not entirely possible to draw a clear line between the two, this is really an argument for using a concept in one area rather than another.) Until we have a clear, if speculative, notion of the connotations of a *genre* class, it is difficult to see how the critic, already besieged by imponderables, could usefully use the term, certainly not as a special term at the root of his analysis. To use the concept in any stronger sense it becomes necessary to establish clearly what film-makers mean when they conceive themselves as making a 'Western'; what limits such a choice may impose on them; in effect, what relationship exists between *auteur* and *genre*. But specific answers to such questions must needs tap the conceptions held by particular film-makers and industries. To methodically analyse the way in which a film-maker utilizes

142

a *genre* for his own purposes (at present a popular critical pursuit) requires that we clearly establish the principal components of *his* conception of the *genre*. But this is not all. The notion that someone utilizes a *genre* suggests something about audience response. It implies that any given film works in such-and-such a way *because* the audience has certain expectations of the *genre*. We can only meaningfully talk of, for instance, an *auteur* breaking the rules of a *genre* if we know what these rules are. And, of course, such rule-breaking has no consequence unless the audience knows as well. Now as I have suggested, *Shane* may well take on its almost 'epic' quality because Stevens for the most part sticks to the rules. In a similar way, *Two Rode Together* and *Cheyenne Autumn* are slightly disconcerting because they break the rules, particularly *vis-à-vis* the Indian/White Man relation. And, most obviously

Rule-breaking: the car in *The Wild Bunch*

in recent years, Peckinpah's 'Westerns' use such elements to disturb the conventional Western universe. The much remarked opening scene of *Ride the High Country* with its policeman and motor cars; the cavalry charging the French Army in *Major Dundee*; the car in *The Wild Bunch*. Now you, the reader, may agree that these are cases of deliberate rule-breaking, and such agreement reflects that there is, in America and much of Europe, some considerable consensus on what constitutes the characteristic 'language' of a Western. But this could well be a special case. To infer from it that all *genre* terms are thus easily employed is hardly justified.

This is not to suggest that *genre* terms are totally useless. It is merely that to employ them requires a much more methodical understanding of the workings of film. And this in turn requires that we specify a set of sociological and psycho-

144

The 'art-movie' genre: Antonioni's *L'Avventura*

logical context assumptions and construct explicit *genre* models within them. If we imagine a general model of the workings of film language, *genre* directs our attention to sublanguages within it. Less centrally, however, the *genre* concept is indispensable in more strictly social and psychological terms as a way of formulating the interplay between culture, audience, films, and film-makers. For example, there is a class of films thought of by a relatively highly-educated, middle-class, group of filmgoers as 'art-movies'. Now for present purposes *genre* is a conception existing in the culture of any particular group or society; it is not a way in which a critic classifies films for methodological purposes, but the much looser way in which an audience classifies its films. On this meaning of the term 'art-movies' is a *genre*. If a culture includes such *genre* notions then, over a period of time, and in a complicated way, certain conventions become established as to what can be expected from an 'art-movie' as compared to some other category. The critics (the 'posh' critics in this case) are mediating factors in such developments. But once such conventions develop they can in turn affect a film-maker's conception of what he is doing. Hence we get a commercial playing up of the 'art-movie' category.

Let me take an impressionistic example bearing in mind that much more extensive work would be needed to establish this in anything more than an intuitive way. At the beginning of the 1960s in this country the general conception of an 'art-movie' revolved around the films of a group of European directors. Bergman was already established with, in particular, *The Seventh Seal* and *Wild Strawberries*. The first year of the new decade had seen Antonioni's *L'Avventura*, Resnais' *Hiroshima mon Amour*, and Fellini's *La Dolce Vita*. These four – though perhaps Resnais less than the others – served to define the 'conventions' of the developing 'art-movies' *genre*. Deliberately and obviously intellectual (there is nothing more deliberate than the final scene of *La Dolce Vita*), with extremely visible individual stylistic characteristics. Bergman's silhouettes, puritan obsessiveness, and grunting Dark Age meals; Antonioni's minimal dialogue, grey photography, and carefully bleak compositions; and Fellini's self-indulgent surrealistic imagery (partly in *La Dolce Vita* but much more clearly in *8½*) circumscribed what was expected of an 'art-movie'. Increasingly, European films, whether 'deliberate' copies (a sub-Antonioni example is Patroni Griffi's *Il Mare*) or later films made by the original directors, met the conventions which the earlier films had established. Antonioni's *Il Deserto Rosso*, Fellini's *Giulietta of the Spirits*, Bergman's *Winter Light* and *The Silence*, are almost stylistic parodies of their director's earlier films. *Giulietta of the Spirits* becomes the ultimate in colour supplement 'art-movies'; a combination of the earlier films and the newly established conventions of the *genre*.

Fellini's $8\frac{1}{2}$

This should serve to illustrate the way in which *genre* notions might constructively be used in tapping the socio-psychological dynamics of film, although it is not designed to convince anyone of the particular case of 'art-movies'. To properly establish such an argument would require detailed research on the changing expectations of 'art-movie' audiences (perhaps via analysis of the 'posh' critics), on the *genre* conceptions (and self-conceptions) held by individuals and groups in various film industries, and on the films themselves. Now there does not seem to me to be any crucial differences between the most commonly employed *genre* term – the 'Western' – and the 'art-movie' category which I have been dealing with. They are both conceptions held by certain groups about certain films. Many of the theoretical problems about using *genre* terms have, however, been overlooked in the case of the 'Western'. It

147

From the 40s (*My Darling Clementine*)...

has become so much a part of our cultural patterning that film criticism has tended to use it as if it were possible to assume common agreement in all the respects on which research would be necessary in the 'art-movie' case. It may be that there is such common agreement on the 'Western'; but it does not follow that this would be true of all *genre* categories. Anyway, it is not at all clear that there is *that* much consensus on the 'Western'. It seems likely that for many people the most Western of Westerns (certainly the most popular if revivals are any indicator) is John Sturges' *The Magnificent Seven*. On the other hand, in the 1940s the same position might be filled by *My Darling Clementine*, in the 1950s by *High Noon*. Conventions change often for reasons entirely out of the control of film-makers and film critics.

In sum, then, *genre* terms seem best immediately employed

... to the 60s (*The Magnificent Seven*)

in the analysis of the relation between groups of films, the
cultures in which they are made, and the cultures in which they
are exhibited. That is, it is a term which can be usefully
employed in relation to a body of knowledge and theory about
the social and psychological context of film. Any assertion we
might make about the use a director makes of *genre* conventions – Peckinpah uses the contrast between our expectations
and actual images to reinforce the 'end of an era' element in
Ride the High Country and *The Wild Bunch* – assumes,
wrongly, the existence of this body of knowledge. To labour the
point, it assumes (1) we know what Peckinpah thinks; (2) we
know what the audience thinks (a) about the films in question,
and (b) about 'Westerns'; (3) Peckinpah knows the answer to
(2(b)) and it is the same as our answer, etc. Most uses of *genre*
effectively *invent* answers to such questions by implicitly claim-

ing to tap some archetypal characteristic of the *genre*, some universal human response. This, as we have seen with Eisenstein, depends on the particular context assumptions employed, and on a more general notion of film language. To leap in with *genre* immediately is to put the cart before the horse.

Critical Methodology
Both *auteur* and *genre* started life deeply implicated in sets of aesthetic judgements. *Auteur* as part of a glorification of the American cinema, a way of looking at trees; *genre* as a condemnation of the American cinema, a way of merging trees into forests. In the course of the 1960s, however, they have become increasingly divorced from this context. Much of their evaluative content has been drained off, leading to their use in an increasingly descriptive sense. Whatever the difficulties and assumptions in their use, and I have tried to show that they are not inconsiderable, they reflect a growing interest in detailed and responsible critical interpretation. The stress on thematic structure in the use of the *auteur* principle has led to an interest in the application to film of methodologies from other disciplines, in particular techniques borrowed from structural linguists and anthropology. The attempt to find a constructive use for *genre* terms has led to an interest in techniques for analysing the recurrent *motifs* in groups of films. Often this has been more concerned with the visual iconography of the *genre*. Either way, thought on film has shifted away from theoretical interests toward discussion of the methodology of analysis. There is now much more self-conscious interest in the processes involved in analysing, comprehending, and evaluating films.

It is much too early to say whether the methodologies under consideration will prove fruitful. Although it seems obviously potentially rewarding to look at the thematic structures implicit in a director's work, the particular structuralist techniques invoked are rarely satisfactory. To reduce the thematic concerns of a group of films to a set of polarities may be adequate in some contexts – consider, for instance, Peter Wollen on Hawks or Alan Lovell on Siegel [13] – but not in others. The assumptions necessary in order to analyse all content in terms of polar opposites are far from safely established. Structures do not 'leap out' from the subject matter as one notable structuralist has suggested; they are at least partly imposed by the consciousness of the observer. Any schematizations produced in this way must, therefore, be treated as hypotheses to be tested against the material, not conclusively established truths. The problems of detailed analysis still remain. The 'structural' method is hardly a magic formula.

Still, such methods have shown some pay-off. The search for otherwise unnoticed patterns, encouraged by the *auteur* principle and the crude application of structural techniques, is not an inconsiderable achievement. It breaks down the regal isolation of the film as basic unit of analysis. Similarly with the use of *genre*, demanding, as it does, that a film or group of films be considered in a larger context. And in the end, *auteur* and *genre* do not retreat into methodology as totally as they initially seem to do. Although they serve to focus our attention predominantly on problems of descriptive analysis, such analysis in turn leads back to theoretical questions. *Aesthetic* issues, because the greater our analysis the greater the invitation to judge or criticize. *Models* of film, because there are no final methodological answers to our problems of understanding. If the *auteur* principle is to be pursued it is not sufficient to pick out the clearest thematic oppositions; to do so risks losing that which makes film specifically *film*. We also need to know how film works, the means of expression at levels other than the narrative surface, in a word, what *language* a film is speaking. It remains to be seen whether semiology (the general science of

13. Peter Wollen, *Signs and Meaning in the Cinema*, Secker and Warburg/British Film Institute, London, 1969, pp. 81–94; Alan Lovell, *Don Siegel – American Cinema, op. cit.*

signs) will provide us with a starter in this respect. It has not started too well. But certainly such demands return us to the interests initially developed by Eisenstein over thirty years ago. If *genre* notions are also to be developed we will inevitably be led to sociological and psychological theories of film, to questions about the context within which the cinema is operating. The form of such questions remains unclear but there is no doubt that they will be asked. Perhaps Eisenstein's self-imposed task of creating a unified theory of film, of understanding the medium in which he was so involved, may yet be completed. If we can escape the aesthetic disputes of the past, and some of the more anti-intellectual prejudices of the present, film theory might yet receive the attention that it merits.

6: Epilogue

In the cause of symmetry a book beginning with an introduction should perhaps end with a conclusion. Rationalist aesthetics, at least, might legitimate such a pattern. But in point of fact it is very difficult to draw any clear and positive conclusions here short of embarking on a further and rather more extensive essay. The only genuine next step would seem to be the development of a body of theories which would deal adequately with the sorts of problems I have been discussing. As a conclusion such a sentiment is merely another introduction. This does not mean that my discussion here has been entirely aimless; future trends in film theory will hardly emerge from an intellectual vacuum. Indeed, the ultimate justification for looking at works of the past must surely be in terms of future utilities – in the widest sense of that much misused term. Anything else trips dangerously close to scholasticism.

In the light of these diffuse reservations, then, my last few pages are by way of epilogue. A concluding chapter but without conclusions. Almost every theme thus far considered has been located specifically in relation to some particular theorist or to some fairly easily recognized tradition. Here, then, I shall try to isolate one or two of the crucial areas which in some sense transcend the disputes and positions with which we have been occupied. As I implied in Chapter One the theorists represented in this book have not a little in common, a fact somewhat obscured in their conventional counter-positioning. Quite obviously the critical concept in this 'common heritage' – though not always explicitly employed – is that of 'language'. This is clearest in Eisenstein and the so-called *auteur* theory where notions variously associated with the idea of a language are absolutely central. Somewhat more subtle, but equally important, is the involvement of language concepts in the classic discussions of realism as both movement and aesthetic. Metz's development of the Bazin tradition in semiological terms is a case in point. And in recent years there has been an increasing willingness to borrow from the expanding discipline of structural linguistics. I do not think that these various usages have been quite as disparate as they might at first appear. Substantively they have differed; but in their *formal* focus we find a strikingly similar set of problems.

To round out my picture of this development, then, I shall take a sketchy look at the growing crystallization of ideas about film language. But in so doing I am conscious of by-passing a further cluster of themes which seem implicitly involved in much contemporary discussion of film. The precise form taken by these developments remains unclear, but the questions with which they are concerned are fairly abstract. What is the nature of theorizing about film? What is its purpose, its relation to other disciplines, and its relevance to problems of evaluation? Interestingly enough, the problems generated in creating a more disciplined analysis of film language increasingly draw attention to these more general issues. We can no doubt expect more and more problems to be thrown up by this area of cross-over. However, a number of these questions seem to me better left until we have mastered less intractable problems. Concern with this philosophic hinterland – what is the nature of film, its art-ness, its film-ness? – seems to me to be presently misplaced. In the long run, of course, it is bound to be important. But in short-run practice these questions are littered with pitfalls which are by no means easy to avoid. Kracauer's failings are a blatantly obvious case of such magnitude that it may be worth curtailing our ambition to avoid such entanglements. For such reasons, among others, it seems more acceptable to focus on 'language' and exclude some of the more traditional areas of aesthetic discourse. Specific strategy depends on what alternatives we have.

Language and Structure

As I have suggested, a loose idea of film language has almost always been part and parcel of the apparatus of film criticism. Anyone whose youthful interests went beyond simply reading film reviews inevitably came across traditional ideas about the 'grammar of film'. The analogy was rarely precise. The 'grammar' of film was usually only a way of organizing discussion in terms of the obvious components of the film process: shot, sequence, cut, and the rest. Although these discussions were not unhelpful they were only superficially theories about the 'language' of film. Only Eisenstein consistently delved deeper. He was interested in the language of film in that he wished to know how and why films communicated 'pathos'. What formal characteristics of the medium produced the required response? In fact he began to develop a poetics based largely on the idea of rhythm, encapsulated in his well-known theory of montage. But he did not approach the study of film language in general, although he occasionally made the mistake of confusing his partial rendering with the whole story. Although he was undoubtedly conscious of the need for a general 'linguistics' of film, and although he had pretensions to theoretical generality, his analysis remained sadly incomplete.

This is hardly a damning criticism. What else was he to do? Even now we have barely delved deeper than Eisenstein with all the armoury of terms borrowed (and stolen) from semiology, structuralism and linguistics. It is even arguable that this very borrowing is only serving to conceal the true nature of our

155

problems beneath a bushel of ambiguities. Certainly these more recent techniques must be used with extreme care lest they fool us into considering the obvious an insight. It also seems helpful — temporarily at least — to try to divorce this structural and linguistic impetus from the critical context within which it has mainly developed. Basically, from the so-called *auteur* theory. Historically, of course, some such structural approach was inevitable in the *auteur* tradition. If one takes as axiomatic the notion that the individual author is the highest common factor in a group of films, then the invitation is to discover the overall structure (of sentiments and styles) which characterize the whole group. Separated from its polemical context, the methods involved in *auteur* analysis lead inevitably to questions of structure, however weakly they may be put. In effect, the patterned relations between themes, styles, and motifs in a director's work are conceived as some kind of reflection of his personal conception of the world, of the structure of his sentiments. Usually an assumed homology of structure between art and artist. And shorn of the term structure there is obviously nothing very new here.

Given that the focus of such weakly 'structural' approaches is on large groups of films, there is no outstanding reason why the principal locus should *always* be the director. Provided the analysis comes up with a common set of characteristics, any further question as to the source of these characteristics remains formally open. For example, it has been customary to ascribe the shared characteristics of a group of 1940s' horror films to their producer Val Lewton, their directors varying. *The Cat People, I Walked with a Zombie, The Leopard Man* by Jacques Tourneur; *The Seventh Victim, Isle of the Dead* by Mark Robson; *The Curse of the Cat People, The Body Snatcher* by Robert Wise. The fact that there intuitively seems to be a series of common concerns in these films has led to some analysis of their common structure, and an additional ascription of this communality to their producer. It never-

156

theless remains that Tourneur's later – and excellent – *Night of the Demon* (also known as *Curse of the Demon*) and Wise's *The Haunting* have not uncommon similarities with the earlier Lewton films, besides a cinematic reference group in the notion of a horror genre. Clearly the horror film, the Western, the thriller – given the difficulties raised in Chapter Five – are all in principle amenable to analysis of structure. The individual artistic persona is not the only possible hypothetical 'explanation' of the existence of a communality of structures across a range of films. A set of genre conventions may be equally apposite.

But this almost purely decoratively terminological use of the notion of structure says little or nothing about the problems of application. This has always been the limitation of straightforward genre or auteur applications. What are the categories of thematic and/or stylistic structure? What class of units are involved? How are they related? Any fully-fledged discussion of film must of necessity deal with such questions, and as a priority. But in the main the 'structuralist' impetus has not yet led to refinement at this level. It has instead given rise to a methodology of analysis based largely on dichotomization; to the idea that culture, thought, or whatever, is innately structured in terms of a series of dichotomies. This has been mainly derived from a vulgarization of the work of Claude Lévi-Strauss, an anthropologist who has proved something of a critical messiah. His analysis of the structure of myth in similar terms has led the unwary to claim 'myth' status for the film genre in modern society. And where application of 'structuralism' has not directly involved such sociological absurdity, it has invariably been simplified in terms of a descending series of dichotomies. Through such techniques it is hoped to render explicit the 'deep' structures of the films in question: what used to be termed in more mundane and facetious manner, the 'hidden meanings'. But of course there is no *a priori* reason for employing dichotomization, particularly when it is assumed –

as it frequently is – that these dichotomically related themes are inherent in the films themselves independent of the observer. Dichotomization can be at best only an epistemological weapon. Its claim to ontological universality is deeply problematic.

In practice a great deal of criticism labelled 'structural' has little to do with this *reductio ad* Lévi-Strauss. It simply reflects some degree of interest in the structure of relationships between thematic clusters in, say, a director's work. And the development of *that* focus was, as we have seen, largely independent of contemporary ideas about 'structuralism'. The act of analysing structure and structural*ism* may usefully be kept separate. Apparently structuralist work, such as Peter Wollen's analysis of Sam Fuller, is only superficially so; a focus on auteur and a desire for method would be sufficient to generate the approach.[1] Indeed, what is valuable about such work is not that it is sufficiently similar to other disciplines to claim some part of their intellectual legitimacy, but that it persists in directing attention toward the notion of structure. It demands that we explicitly look at the film(s) as a total configuration rather than a discrete set of elements. But basically it tells us little more. It does not, as it stands, seriously address itself to the problem of film language, of how films in fact communicate these various allegedly structured clusters. In this context other associated inputs have proved more interesting, if not yet more lucrative.

The model for this much more specified interest in film language has been linguistics. Thus, there has been a suggestion that it might be possible to create a cinematic equivalent to Chomsky's transformational grammar. Such a theory would enable us to generate all possible grammatical statements in the 'language'. But this hope leans heavily on the possibility of analogous development, a faith which may be misplaced.

1. See Peter Wollen, 'Notes towards a Structural Analysis of the Films of Samuel Fuller', *Cinema*, 1, Dec. 1968.

Perhaps the non-cognitive element is so important in film (along with most other arts) that linguistic strategies are too cognitively oriented for constructive application. It is a little too early to know, but even Bernstein's now familiar distinction between restricted and elaborated codes has a suspiciously cognitive bias. Applications, as opposed to programmatic suggestions, have not been common. More often than not 'linguistic' inclinations have manifested themselves in relation to semiology, the general science of signs. But again, we have yet to see a developed semiological mode in relation to film. Writers on the subject have often been basically more concerned to illumine the ontological nature of film as a stage in developing an aesthetic position. Metz, in one guise or another, develops and reiterates versions of Bazin's classic position.[2] And while Wollen makes illuminating *general* use of Peirce's distinction between iconic, indexical, and symbolic signs, the traditional semiological focus on the symbolic or arbitrary sign prevents us from adequately filling in the detail.[3] And reference to Barthes' works is demonstration of the stringent limitations on semiological analysis of more complex communication systems.[4]

We are then relatively well provided with sources of 'linguistic' sensitization, but little more. Excellent cases have been made for focusing on the persistent structures running through one or a series of films. By and large, however, this interest has developed in relation to theme at the expense of style; needless to say there is no reason to think of this as a necessary con-

---

2. See, among many others, Christian Metz, 'Le dire et le dit au cinéma: vers le déclin d'un vraisemblable', *Communications*, 11, 1968; 'Propositions méthodologiques pour l'analyse du film', *Social Science Information*, VII, 4, 1968.
3. Peter Wollen, *Signs and Meaning in the Cinema*, Secker & Warburg/BFI, London, 1969, pp. 120ff.
4. Roland Barthes, *Elements of Semiology* and *Writing Degree Zero*, both published by Jonathan Cape, London, 1967.

junction, though style is undoubtedly more difficult to handle. But a clear prerequisite, if 'structural' analysis is to be anything more than a dressed up list of dichotomous distinctions, must be the development of a detailed theory of film language. Whether this will derive from a general science of signs or will later be slotted into it remains open. Most likely both strategies will be involved in some part. But at the moment all we really have is an *a priori* faith derived partly from the respectable overtones of terms like 'structuralism' and 'semiology'. As far as film criticism is concerned both labels are still getting by on credit. They constitute very general pointers in the direction of 'progress' but have thus far shown little real analytical power. Naïve structuralism especially might be argued to have had predominantly negative consequences in reducing analysis to a formula simplification of a few themes. And none of the major contemporary approaches have come to terms with the particular structured relations which were of so much interest to Eisenstein: rhythm, tempo, and formal compositional contrast. Undoubtedly there is promise but it remains largely unfulfilled. We have only a few fragmentary clues as to our best directions of development.

Theories of Film
It is a commonplace to suggest that all processes of comprehension involve a framework of assumptions, propositions, and the like. Attempts to evaluate the aesthetic importance of an object as much as attempts to empirically investigate it are basically processes of 'mapping' the object into some previously constituted framework. Neither endeavour exists in a vacuum. Of course, nothing follows as such from this observation: several further premises are needed for that. But it does seem that experience in other areas of inquiry suggests that there are important payoffs to be derived from explicit discussion of such frameworks. Their nature, their internal consistency, and the manner of their relation to their subject. For facts do not

L'Année Dernière a Marienbad

speak for themselves and aesthetic judgements are hardly self-evident. If this is true, then a concern with theories of film is not simply a decorative addendum to the real thing. On the contrary, we *must* know about the theories lest we confuse a necessarily partial theoretical account with 'absolute truth', or, more familiarly, absolute canons of beauty. *Explicit* theorizing is essential. Without it we simply dissolve our studies into a series of variously recognized prejudices.

Given this general point there still remain many alternative strategies within the rubric 'theory'. We have looked at some of the more exemplary cases: Bazin, Kracauer, Grierson, Eisenstein. But is it possible to single out any particular line of theoretical development as presently most potentially rewarding? It will be clear to the reader who has got this far that I am not without belief in such a thread. Loosely conceived, film 'language' seems as good a label as any. The basic reasoning in favour of such a focus is straightforward. Though our studies may be directed at many things — the relation of film to social change; the psychological appeal of genre; the bases for a set of aesthetic criteria; and endless others — whatever the aim we come up against one persistent problem: how to tap the meaning of the film(s). Not in the very specific sense of that term; not in the 'What does *L'Année Dernière à Marienbad* mean?' idiom. Meaning in the sense of raising questions about the ways in which language is used, the form of recurring patterns, the incidence of unlikely absences, the contextual significance of the film, and so on. Trying to make sense of the narrative thread is only one element in the range of levels of meaning involved. Whatever our specific interests — and as I have said they may be many — the core problem lies in analysis of 'meaning'.

So, improving our understanding of the ways in which film may be meaningful is a priority; any further analysis must needs build on this foundation. This is patently obvious in areas of contextual interest. Most commonly in sociology and psychology. Whatever linkage the social scientist is exploring inevitably derives in some respect from an understanding of the meaning of the films in question. Even rampant behaviourism has some such covert point of reference. The intermediary connecting human action and aesthetic object is always some generalized notion of meaning. And elsewhere the importance of meaning is not unclear. Aesthetic evaluation, for instance, invariably has reference to particular patterns which are meaningful in certain aesthetically prescribed ways. It is quite apparent — even from the limited materials discussed in this book — that assumptions about the manner in which films are meaningful (about 'language') are very basic indeed. Not a few of the problems we have been discussing derive from questionable assumptions at this level. In this area we really need renewed theoretical and analytical energies.

It is partly for these reasons that Eisenstein might be

reconsidered. In some areas at least he made a good start. Unfortunately much of his theoretical contribution to the solution of such problems has been sunk without trace in the backwaters of Realism. The image of Eisenstein as formalist has dominated. In some ways this is deeply ironical. It does seem that a number of the problems found in the theoretical developments of the realism position derive from misunderstandings in just the areas toward which Eisenstein points. Take the contortions discussed in Chapter Four. The core of the tangle, for both Bazin and Kracauer, lies in the relation between particular elements of cinematic language and conventions about the 'real'. Bazin appears to have been aware of this, though he fails to push it through to any single conclusion. Instead he remains ambivalent, in the end postulating two contradictory realist 'essences'. If Eisenstein's proper impetus had not been subsequently sidetracked the realist aestheticians might not have found themselves in such a mess. They have much to answer for.

Three epilogic conclusions then. First and foremost we must theorize. Otherwise our knowledge will simply stultify at its present primitive state. Secondly, in theorizing we would be better advised to try to explore what *is* for a while instead of arguing about what *ought* to be: *models* rather than *aesthetics*. And lastly, *models* of film language must be a first priority. With resources scarce this seems to be not just the best investment, but ultimately the only available possibility. As we have seen earlier in this chapter recent years have brought a number of shifts in this direction. The combination of the classical theories I have been considering here along with these later inputs seems at least a promising beginning. Let us hope it will lead to a promising end.

164

Bibliography

This bibliography includes all materials referred to directly in the text as well as further relevant references.

Anderson, Lindsay, 'British Cinema: the Descending Spiral', *Sequence*, 7, 1949.

Anderson, Lindsay, 'Stand Up! Stand Up!', *Sight and Sound*, 1956.

Armes, Roy, 'A Polemic', *Screen*, 10, 6, 1969.

Arnheim, Rudolf, *Art and Visual Perception*, Faber and Faber, London, 1956.

Arnheim, Rudolf, *Film as Art*, Faber and Faber, London, 1958.

Arnheim, Rudolf, *Toward a Psychology of Art*, Faber and Faber, London, 1956. 2nd ed. 1966; Berkeley, University of California Press.

Balazs, Bela, *Theory of the Film*, Dennis Dobson, London, 1952.

Barthes, Roland, *Elements of Semiology*, Jonathan Cape, London, 1967.

Barthes, Roland, *Mythologies*, Jonathan Cape, London, 1972.

Barthes, Roland, *Writing Degree Zero*, Jonathan Cape, London, 1967.

Bazin, André, 'Evolution du Western', *Cahiers du Cinéma*, December, 1955.

Bazin, André, *Qu'est-ce que le Cinéma? I. Ontologie et Langage*, Editions du Cerf, Paris, 1958.

Bazin, André, *Qu'est-ce que le Cinéma? II. Le Cinéma et les autres Arts*, Editions du Cerf, Paris, 1959.

Bazin, André, *Qu'est-ce que le Cinéma? III. Cinéma et Sociologie*, Editions du Cerf, Paris, 1961.

Bazin, André, *Qu'est-ce que le Cinéma? IV. Une Esthétique de la Réalité*, Editions du Cerf, Paris, 1962.

Bazin, André, *What is Cinema?*, University of California Press, Berkeley and Los Angeles, 1967.

Bazin, André, *What is Cinema?*, Vol. 2, University of California Press, Berkeley and Los Angeles, 1971.

Eisenstein, Sergei, *Film Essays*, Dennis Dobson, London, 1968.

Eisenstein, Sergei, *Film Form*, New York, Harcourt, Brace, 1949; Dennis Dobson, London, 1951.

Eisenstein, Sergei, *Notes of a Film Director*, Lawrence & Wishart, London, 1959; rev. ed. New York, Dover Publications, 1970.

Eisenstein, Sergei, *The Film Sense*, Faber & Faber, London, 1943; New York, Meridian Books, 1957.

Hall, Stuart ; Whannel, Paddy, *The Popular Arts*, Hutchinson Educational, London, 1964.

Hardy, Forsyth (ed.), *Grierson on Documentary*, Collins, London, 1946.

Hardy, Forsyth (ed.), *Grierson on Documentary*, Faber & Faber, London, 1966; New York, Praeger, 1971.

Huaco, George A., *The Sociology of Film Art*, Basic Books, New York, 1965.

Kael, Pauline, 'Is there a cure for Film Criticism? or: Some Unhappy Thoughts on Siegfried Kracauer's *Nature of Film: the Redemption of Physical Reality*', *Sight and Sound*, 31, 2, 1962.

Kael, Pauline, *I Lost it at the Movies*, Boston; Toronto; Little, Brown & Co., 1965; Jonathan Cape, London, 1966.

Kitses, Jim, *Horizons West*, Thames & Hudson/British Film Institute, London, 1969. (Cinema One).

Kracauer, Siegfried, 'National Types as Hollywood Presents Them', *Public Opinion Quarterly*, 13, 1949.

Kracauer, Siegfried, *From Caligari to Hitler*: A Psychological History of the German Film, Princeton University Press, Princeton, 1947.

Kracauer, Siegfried, *Theory of Film: the Redemption of Physical Reality*, Oxford University Press, New York, 1965.

Lawson, John Howard, *Film: the Creative Process*, Hill & Wang, New York, 1964.

Lindgren, Ernest, *The Art of the Film*, Allen & Unwin, London, 1948.

Lovell, Alan, 'Robin Wood – A dissenting View', *Screen*, 10, 2, 1969.

Lovell, Alan, 'The Common Pursuit of True Judgment', *Screen*, 11, 4/5, 1970.

Lovell, Alan, *Don Siegel – American Cinema*, BFI Education Department, London, 1968.

MacCann, Richard Dyer (ed.), *Film: a Montage of Theories*, E. P. Dutton, New York, 1966.

Metz, Christian, 'Le Cinéma: Langue ou Langage', *Communications*, 4, 1964.

166

Metz, Christian, 'Le dire et le dit au cinéma: vers le déclin d'un vraisemblable', *Communications*, 11, 1968.

Metz, Christian, 'La Grande Syntagmatique du Film Narratif', *Communications*, 8, 1966.

Metz, Christian, 'Propositions Methodologiques pour l'analyse du film', *Social Science Information*, VII, 4, 1968. In English in *Screen*, 114, 1/2, 1973.

Metz, Christian, *Essais sur la signification au cinéma*, Editions Klincksieck, Paris, Vol. 1, 1968, Vol. 2.

Metz, Christian, *Langage et Cinéma*, Larousse, Paris, 1971.

Nizhny, Vladimir, *Lessons with Eisenstein*, Allen & Unwin, London, 1962.

Pryluck, C., 'Structural analysis of Motion Pictures as a Symbol System', *Journalism Quarterly*, 16, 4, 1968.

Pryluck, C., and Snow, R. E., 'Towards a Psycholinguistics of Cinema', *AV Communications Review*, XV, 1, 1967.

Pudovkin, Vsevolod, *Film Technique and Film Acting*, Vision Press, London, 1953; Mayflower, 1958.

Sarris, Andrew, 'Notes on the Auteur Theory in 1962', *Film Culture*, 27, 1962–3.

Sarris, Andrew, *The American Cinema*, E. P. Dutton, New York, 1968.

Seton, Marie, *Sergei M. Eisenstein*, London, Bodley Head, 1952; Grove Press, New York, 1960.

Spottiswoode, Raymond, *A Grammar of Film*, Faber & Faber, London, 2nd ed. 1955; Berkeley, University of California Press, 1950.

Talbot, Daniel (ed.), *Film: an Anthology*, New York, Simon and Schuster, 1959; pbk. and shortened ed. California University Press, Berkeley, 1966.

Tudor, Andrew, 'Genre: Theory and Mispractice in Film Criticism', *Screen*, 11, 6, 1970.

Wollen, Peter, 'Notes Towards a Structural Analysis of the Films of Samuel Fuller', *Cinema*, 1, 1968.

Wollen, Peter, *Signs and Meaning in the Cinema*, Secker & Warburg/BFI, London, 1969. (Cinema One); 2nd ed. (revised), 1973.

Wollen, Peter (ed.), *Working Papers on the Cinema: Sociology and Semiology*, British Film Institute, London, 1969.

Wood, Robin, 'Ghostly Paradigm and H.C.F.: An Answer to Alan Lovell', *Screen*, 10, 3, 1969.

Wood, Robin, *Hitchcock's Films*, Zwemmer, London; New York, A. S. Barnes 1965; 2nd ed. 1969.

Wood, Robin, *Howard Hawks*, Secker & Warburg/BFI, London, 1968. (Cinema One).

Acknowledgements

I would like to express my gratitude to a number of people. To Peter Wollen with whose help the original idea of the book was developed. To Alan Lovell, Terry Lovell, and Christopher Williams, who were all kind enough to read the manuscript and comment on it in detail. They were more helpful than they realize. To Marion Haberhauer whose secretarial aid was impeccable. To Min Tudor whose general help was invaluable.

This book is in memory of Phaedra and Myshkin.

Stills by courtesy of British Lion, CIC, Columbia, Connoisseur, Contemporary, Gala, M-G-M, Paramount, Rank, RKO, 20th Century-Fox, United Artists, Universal, Warner Bros., and the Stills Library of the National Film Archive, London.